Secrets
of
Ruth

Secrets of Ruth

A Devotional for Women

Patricia Mitchell

BARBOUR
PUBLISHING

© 2015 by Barbour Publishing

Print ISBN 978-1-64352-940-0

eBook Editions:
Adobe Digital Edition (.epub) 978-1-63609-211-9
Kindle and MobiPocket Edition (.prc) 978-1-63609-212-6

Devotional writing and compilation by Patricia Mitchell in association with Snapdragon Group℠, Tulsa, OK.

Published by Barbour Publishing, Inc., 1810 Barbour Drive, Uhrichsville, Ohio 44683, www.barbourbooks.com

Our mission is to inspire the world with the life-changing message of the Bible.

Member of the
Evangelical Christian
Publishers Association

Printed in the United States of America.

Contents

The Secrets of Ruth

"Wherever you go, I will go." These words have graced pledges of lifelong commitment ever since Ruth uttered them nearly three thousand years ago. Yet there's far more in her promise than a heartwarming ideal. Uncover the layers of meaning in these words and you will find that they belong on the lips of everyone who desires a closer, more intimate, and more vibrant relationship with God.

The biblical book of Ruth is a story of family loyalty, spiritual integrity, and romantic love. Its themes of tenderness and devotion, kindness and commitment still resonate today. As you read, you no doubt will recognize many challenges that have touched your own life—grief and loss, unwelcome change and practical necessity. Discover, in addition, inspiring examples of faithfulness applied to real-life decisions, despite the pull of personal preference. In Ruth, see how respect and decency were applied to common business dealings, even though, then as now, self-interest was the norm.

The reflections in *Secrets of Ruth* are based on themes from the book of Ruth. Introduced by a passage from scripture, each reading highlights a recognizable, down-to-earth circumstance that's relevant to our lives today, coupled with God's divine response. See how God uses common events to bring His people closer to Him, and watch how He makes His will known through the faith He plants in the human heart. Celebrate the promise of the Messiah that God fulfilled through Ruth's descendants. Celebrate too His promise of continuing love that He showers on you today.

Where you go I will go,
and where you stay I will stay.
Your people will be my people
and your God my God.

Ruth 1:16 NIV

PART I:

Naomi and Ruth

Famine Strikes

*Before Israel was ruled by kings, Elimelech from
the tribe of Ephrath lived in the town of Bethlehem.
His wife was named Naomi, and their two sons were
Mahlon and Chilion. But when their crops failed,
they moved to the country of Moab.*

RUTH 1:1–2 CEV

Famine! To this day, storms, drought, infestation, and warfare in parts of the world force growers off their land. Their crops lost, they and everyone in the community dependent on them have no food for the table. If they can, they move to another place and start all over again.

For most of us, however, starvation is a scourge witnessed through the lens of a TV camera. Our lands yield crops, and our market shelves are well stocked with goods of all kinds. Yet we know famine. We experience it when our source of income vanishes because of job loss, a stock market reversal, or a failed business; when the love, affection, and emotional support we depend on disappears with the passing of a loved one; or when our hopes for the future crumble in the wake of a devastating medical diagnosis. Famine forces us to make a move—emotionally, spiritually, and sometimes physically.

It's famine that spurred Elimelech, his wife, and his sons to settle in Moab, a nation east of the Dead Sea. Though necessary, the decision was a painful one. Far from family and friends, these God-fearing Israelites would find themselves living among idol-worshippers with a reputation for decadence and immorality. This certainly was not what the couple had planned and most assuredly not where they had hoped to raise their sons. Yet when they left Bethlehem for this foreign land, God went with them. They took courage in knowing that He is not confined to a place but dwells in the hearts of those who love Him.

Have you ever been compelled to pick up stakes and settle in a new place? Perhaps changes in your health or relationships have turned your plans for the future completely upside down. Maybe a desire to delve deeper into God's purpose for you has started you on a journey toward greater spiritual maturity and deeper understanding. In times like these, "famine" is taking you from known to unknown, from old to new.

Though circumstances can move you away from places and people you love, they can never move you away from God. In Him, you have the strength to continue, an abundance of comfort, and a rich supply of possibilities. He is yours, and you are His wherever you go.

Dear God, thank You for the assurance of Your presence wherever I am. Let loss and dislocation, whether physical or emotional, serve only to move me closer to You, the Source of everything I really need. Help all who suffer famine find their hope, comfort, and abundance in You. Amen.

Choices to Make

In those days Israel had no king;
everyone did as they saw fit.

JUDGES 21:25 NIV

The story of Ruth takes place in a time very similar to our own. In the land of Canaan, God's people lived alongside unbelieving tribes. The easygoing, pleasure-seeking, and human-centered ways of the Canaanites drew many Israelites away from God's commandments. Political unrest, culture clashes, and intermittent battles produced social upheaval and the deterioration of authority. Greed and selfishness ran rampant, time-honored values were questioned, the suffering of others was ignored, and lives were given over to frivolous pursuits. Yet then as now, there were those who remained faithful to God.

Elimelech and Naomi held to their faith and the faith of their ancestors. Like us, they were surrounded by many strong influences and may have wondered at times if their pious ways kept them from some of the good things of life. Was it necessary to observe the Sabbath when others of their community rarely attended worship? Were God's guidelines for personal behavior still relevant in this day and age? We can imagine Elimelech speculating if honesty was really the best policy as he watched his cunning neighbors prosper or as Naomi was tempted to join the women gathered around the well exchanging gossip instead of seeing to the needs of her household.

Naomi and Elimelech had choices to make, and so do we. We're not immune from the appeal of going along with what feels comfortable rather than what we know is the right thing to do. Our eyes can't help but observe friends, neighbors, and coworkers living without so much as a nod to God's ways, and we wonder if we're losing out by paying attention to His rules and guidelines. We have a choice: follow God or follow the crowd; lean on Him or rely on our own understanding; give of ourselves to others or take from others for ourselves. We can live as we see fit or as God would have us live.

Your world, your society, and perhaps even members of your own family challenge you to remain faithful to God. As God's child, you might feel like a stranger dwelling in a strange land, even though you've been living in the same place for years. Scorn or ridicule may come your way because of your faith. Each time this happens, your choice matters. It matters to God because He cares about you. It matters to you because standing up for God's ways strengthens your faith. It matters to others because they're influenced by the things you say and do. What choices have you made lately?

Heavenly Father, grant me strength and courage to remain hopeful in a tumultuous world, faithful to Your ways, and helpful to those around me. Through the work of Your Spirit in my heart, let my choices reflect my love for You and my willingness to follow where You lead. Amen.

Family Life

Elimelech, the husband of Naomi, died, and she was left with her two sons. These took Moabite wives; the name of the one was Orpah and the name of the other Ruth.

RUTH 1:3–4 ESV

*N*aomi must have felt the disappointment keenly. Here the two sons of devout, observant Jewish parents chose to marry outside the faith. As the wedding ceremonies were taking place, she may have regretted staying so long in Moab. If the boys had been raised in Bethlehem, surely they would have chosen wives among the young women in their community. If they had listened to her advice before committing themselves, the three of them could have made the journey back to the land of their birth. But it was too late now. See Naomi's face turn away, her eyes moist with tears.

Families are like that. They're made up of people bonded together in relationship, yet individuals with their own hopes and dreams, affections, and aspirations. And often there's one—or two—who just don't fit in. It could be an adult child who rejects the faith he was so lovingly brought up in; an aunt or cousin who always seems to stir up controversy and ill feelings; an in-law from another background, with other values, accustomed to different foods, friends, and expectations. Naomi's new family resembled many of ours today.

No matter what Naomi felt in her heart, however, she accepted her sons' wives. As we'll see, Naomi welcomed Ruth and Orpah into the family and treated them with warmth and kindness. From events that follow, we know that a deep friendship developed among the three women, despite their differences in age, upbringing, and religion. Naomi remained faithful to her Lord, not simply in thought and word but in action. Her daughters-in-law couldn't fail but notice that there was something divinely different about this woman from Bethlehem. At what point they began to ask Naomi about the God of the Israelites, we don't know. But we do know that Naomi's answers to their questions planted a seed in their hearts; and in the heart of Ruth, the seed took root.

God may have brought people into your family or into your social circle for a very special purpose. It's so they can experience your patience, generosity, kindness, and unconditional love and hear the words that His Spirit will use to plant the seed of faith in their hearts. Perhaps someone's face or name has popped into your mind. Ask God to show you how you can share His love with those who are close to you.

Almighty God, please send the gift of Your Holy Spirit into my heart so my words and actions will reflect Your love for all people. Grant me wisdom to answer when others ask the reason for my faith, and bless me with the privilege of planting seeds for You. Amen.

Everything's Happening

L ife goes on! Things quieted down after the wedding festivities were over. With Ruth and Orpah moved into their husbands' home, Naomi and her daughters-in-law now faced the practical matter of running the house. There were seeds to plant, loaves of bread to bake, fruit to pick, stews to stir, meals to serve, bundles of flax to dry, stalks to weave, cloaks to mend, bedding to freshen, floors to sweep, and visiting friends and guests to shower with hospitality. Then as now, the one who does what has the potential to disrupt family life, sour relationships, and foster years of anger and resentment.

As the matriarch, Naomi took charge of the household. It was her responsibility not only to divide the chores but also to set the tone of the relationship with her daughter-in-law. Her attitude would set the standard, and the way she spoke to Ruth and Orpah would be the way they would speak to each other. From the start, Naomi divided daily tasks fairly, not sparing herself part of the work. She proved willing to teach and help, and her compassion for the emotional comfort and well-being of the younger women created a relationship of mutual respect and genuine affection. Because of Naomi's commitment to kindness, a home that could have been filled with tension, jealousy, and unhappiness instead became an oasis of joy, peace, and contentment.

Each of us influences our homes, communities, and workplaces by the way we treat those around us. Our daily routine offers unique opportunities to nurture our relationships, practice kindness, speak gently, and help others grow in spiritual knowledge and understanding. Consistent commitment to kindness enables the bonds of family and friendship to take root, grow strong, and withstand the test of time.

Far from unimportant, routine responsibilities allow us to treat ourselves with kindness too. We can take satisfaction in doing small things well and find contentment in the blessings God has showered on us this day. In peaceful, uneventful times, we have more opportunity to nurture our spirit, develop our highest thoughts, cultivate our best qualities, plan for the future, and think deeply about the things that really matter. It might be said that when we think nothing is happening, in fact everything is happening.

If God has blessed you with a period of peace right now, how are you using it? How are your attitude and perspective lifting the tone of your home or workplace? Are there friendships you can strengthen, interests you can pursue, simple pleasures you can enjoy? Let everything start happening now!

---

*Dear God, thank You for times of peace and tranquility
I have experienced. Let me use these special times to enrich
my life and the lives of those around me so we will be better
able to meet life's difficulties with patience, courage,
endurance, and most of all, faith. Amen.*

Limited Options

*Then both Mahlon and Chilion also died; so the
woman survived her two sons and her husband.*

RUTH 1:5 NKJV

The meaning of their names suggests that they suffered ill health.
Though we don't know how long Mahlon and Chilion were
married, the fact that neither Ruth nor Orpah conceived might be
attributed to an infirmity. Perhaps ill health led to their untimely
deaths, and it may not have been a surprise. But as with the passing
of those we love, it was heartbreaking.

Not only did Naomi, Ruth, and Orpah lose beloved sons and
husbands, they also lost their means of support. Their options were
limited to begging for food, prostituting themselves for money, or
relying on the charity of others to support them. Not one of these
could have sounded appealing to the women!

We too can find ourselves faced with a number of uninviting
options. Family responsibilities, inadequate skills or education,
past poor choices, emotional disorders, economic restrictions, and
physical disabilities are some of the stark realities that limit options.
Some of us can and do reach high, overcome limitations, and meet
extraordinary goals—give God the glory! But for others among us,
such a feat is not possible. There comes the day we step into the
food pantry and ask for a bag of groceries. We admit that we can't

manage on our own and ask for help. We accept assistance, despite what we had once thought of "those people."

A time of utmost physical or spiritual need is a time of extraordinary blessing. At these times and these times alone, we're forced to lay aside self-pride and self-reliance, coming to terms with the undeniable fact that we aren't all-wise, all-knowing, all-powerful. Things aren't working out, and we have nowhere to turn! No good options, no alternative we can fall back on! We've hit bottom, and we know it. So now we're ready to turn from ourselves to God, who has been waiting for us all along.

Like Naomi, who humbly and prayerfully faced the limited options available to her, we have no need to spend time in denial, excuse making, or blaming others for our predicament. No matter what happened, this is our reality. It's not pretty, for sure. At least it's not pretty to us because we can't see what God has in mind for our future.

When all feasible options seem less than satisfactory, take your situation to your Lord in prayer. Think, meditate, and consider where He may want you to go from here, and know He will be with you as you make perhaps a difficult, but God-pleasing, choice.

Lord God, many times I'm unhappy with the options available to me. Grant me the courage to make the best choice when I must and the insight to discover something new, something better in it. In everything, let what I do fall into place for me, according to Your will. Amen.

Daily Bread

Naomi heard in Moab that the LORD had blessed his
people in Judah by giving them good crops again.

RUTH 1:6 NLT

With all the bad news Naomi, Ruth, and Orpah had received lately, finally a morsel of good news came their way. They heard that the long-standing famine finally had broken in Bethlehem. For Naomi, the development provided another option: she could go back to Bethlehem. Although far from the optimistic, confident married mother of two sons her relatives had last seen, she could return to her extended family. Surely they would do their duty and provide for her simple needs. It was a bittersweet blessing, of course. Relying on others was not what she ever expected to have to do; but she thanked God anyway. He is the source of all food!

The need for physical sustenance led Naomi back to Bethlehem, and the need for spiritual sustenance leads us to God. While God fed Naomi's soul with the promise of a Messiah to come, He feeds us today with the now-fulfilled promise in the life, death, and resurrection of His Son Jesus Christ. God strengthens and nourishes us with spiritual daily bread each time we come to Him with humble, believing hearts.

Through the activity of His Spirit within us, He comforts us in our sorrows, supports us in our struggles, and opens our eyes to the lasting joy of belonging to Him. He forgives our sins when we come to Him for forgiveness, restores our spiritual health, enables us to know and do His will, assures of His presence, and grants us genuine peace. What good news to come our way because this is the kind of bread our souls crave every day!

Do you feel spiritually malnourished? Are you hungry for the good food He has to offer? Then hear the Good News. As a beloved daughter of God, you are a member of His family, and His Son Jesus Christ has made it His duty to feed you. Read and hear what He wants to tell you in scripture because that's where He has promised to nourish your soul and meet your deepest needs. Pray, trusting Him to give you the sustenance He knows will uphold and strengthen you. Follow Him, relying on your Lord and Savior to lead you into a land of good and abundant crops. Come with confidence because He will not turn you away! He has invited you to His feast, and there is a place at His table for you.

I thank You, Lord Jesus Christ, for Your goodness in providing the food I need most—food for my soul. Lead me to Your table where You offer wholesome food for my faith, lasting peace for my heart, and rich nourishment for my Spirit-given willingness to do Your will. Amen.

Decision Time

Naomi and her daughters-in-law got ready to leave
Moab to return to her homeland.

RUTH 1:6 NLT

*D*epressed, bereft of resources, and far from home, Naomi was not in a happy situation. If she were to stay in Moab, she would have to depend fully on the kindness of strangers and spend her old age among those whose first priority would be their own families. Yet at least she would not have to bear the pity of people she had grown up with. If she were to go back to Bethlehem, she still would have to rely on charity, humbling herself in front of those among her relatives who had prospered. There her support was more assured, however, since family members, by Israel's laws, were obliged to care for those among them who were in need. So when she learned that the famine had ended and better economic times might prompt the generosity and goodwill of her relatives, she considered the idea of returning to the place of her birth.

The hours of anguished prayer and earnest deliberating that Naomi surely experienced are like our own when we come to life's crossroads. Go this way or that way? Each direction has its pros and cons. Either way could be God's will, for neither involves any actions contrary to His commandments. Both stand up to the tests of mature reasoning, responsible thinking, and personal viability. As we will discover, Naomi weighed her own interests against the interests of her beloved daughters-in-law. Although she felt the bitterness of leaving them and the friends she had made among the Moabite women, her real position was inescapable: she was not one of them. If hard times came in Moab, she might be left to starve, too old to make the journey back home. Her place was in Bethlehem. And so, putting the days to come in God's hands, she made her decision, announced her intentions, and set out for the land of her birth.

God will not always provide a clear yes or no to the decisions you face in life. How simple for you if He would! Instead He asks you to trust Him with your future. He gives you whatever wisdom and resources, advice and abilities you need to make the choice that will lead you closer to Him and enable you to do His will.

Are you at a crossroads today? Talk to Him about both directions. Get the best advice available to you, and consider your viable options. Decide on one. Don't look back, but trust Him with your way ahead.

Heavenly Father, help me use the information, resources, and wisdom I possess to make the best decisions for my life and for the lives of those dependent on me. Once I have decided, I put the days into Your hands, trusting You to guide my steps and bless my way. Amen.

Yes or No?

She started out from the place she had been living,
she and her two daughters-in-law with her,
on the road back to the land of Judah.

RUTH 1:7 MSG

Ruth and Orpah, in traveling with Naomi, may have intended to live with her in Bethlehem. Or they may have been extending to their mother-in-law the courtesy of accompanying her for some distance, a common custom at the time. Either way, their love and respect for her is obvious. They surely understood why Naomi would want to return to her former home, but the hard facts could not lessen their sorrow.

The conversation along the road—can you hear it? Memories of Mahlon and Chilion, and their family times together; expressions of gratitude for the home they had found with one another; the forced smiles through the tears as each woman tried to remain brave and cheerful for the sake of the others. Every footstep they took on the road to Judah, however, was a step closer to the point where there would be no turning back.

Naomi had taken such a journey in the opposite direction a decade earlier. Then, she was the one leaving her homeland and going to a foreign place. Now Ruth and Orpah were the ones leaving their homeland of Moab, their families and friends, and everything familiar to them since childhood. As their town drew smaller and smaller behind them, their feelings ranged from anticipation to hesitation, from certainty to misgivings, from resolve to doubt that they had made the right decision. Whether they planned to part with Naomi several hours into the journey or go with her to Bethlehem, now they must decide for sure.

Their emotions were like ours when we're on the verge of a life-changing and irrevocable decision. Though at first we might feel excited about this new stage in life, as the day of "departure" begins to dawn, its reality closes in. So we're *really* going to move. . . marry. . .have a baby. . .retire? Memories flood our thoughts, and we feel the sting of saying goodbye to our loved ones; of giving up our independence to begin a new life with another person; of assuming the responsibilities of motherhood; of leaving the familiar structure and support of the workaday world.

Spiritual partings are no less startling and no less real. Perhaps you have experienced them—and if you haven't, you will! It's when following God's guidelines means you will need to make a break with the past. Will you say yes to going forward spiritually, or no? Ruth and Orpah needed to decide. How about you?

Dear Lord, when You lead me out of my comfort zone and I leave familiar landscapes, habits, and lifestyles behind, grant me the wisdom, discernment, fortitude, and will to make the right decision. Show me the way when I wander, and strengthen my resolve when I waver. Amen.

When Love Shows

Naomi said to her two daughters-in-law, "Go back, each of you, to your mother's home. May the Lord show you kindness, as you have shown kindness to your dead husbands and to me. May the Lord grant that each of you will find rest in the home of another husband."

RUTH 1:8–9 NIV

The moment of parting had come. In the God of Israel's name, Naomi blessed Ruth and Orpah, and she prayed that He would richly reward these Moabite widows for the years of kindness they had shown herself and her sons. She prayed also that they would again know the dignity and security that a new marriage could bring them. "Now, go back home," she said.

Naomi's counsel was well founded. Wanting the best for Ruth and Orpah, she urged the young women to return to their families, where marriage and children were still a possibility. The chance of two foreign widows finding husbands in Israel was slim, but among their own people, it could happen. While Ruth and Orpah's continued company would have pleased and benefited Naomi, she put the interests of her beloved daughters-in-law ahead of her own.

Genuine love like Naomi's is selfless love. When we truly love others, we want the best for them, and we're willing to put aside our own interests and preferences for the sake of their well-being. We show it when we go out of our way to please the one we love;

when we give of our time and resources to our children; when we do everything we can for our friends to show them how much we care about them. Always easy? Always convenient? Always without a sacrifice on our part? Of course not. But genuine love isn't thinking of me first; it's thinking of you.

In His love, God put us first when He sent His Son Jesus into the world. His love compelled Jesus, true God and true man, to walk among us, illustrating God's great compassion for us by healing the sick, accepting the poor and the outcasts, and teaching all who would listen how to live according to God's will. Selflessly, Jesus paid the ultimate price for us by dying for our sins because this is something we could not do for ourselves. His resurrection proves His power over all life and His living love for us.

When you see selfless love at work, you're seeing God at work. Your acts of selfless love to others grant you the divine privilege of knowing what it's like to really care, really cherish—really love.

Dear God, thank You for the extraordinary love You have shown me through the selfless life, sacrificial death, and triumphant resurrection of Jesus Christ. Let my response of gratitude be nothing less than a life marked by acts of visible, practical, and faithful love to others. Amen.

Travel Time

Naomi kissed them. They cried and said,
"We want to go with you and live among your people."

RUTH 1:9–10 CEV

Robbers hid in caves and coves along the dusty road, ready to prey on vulnerable passersby. In all likelihood, the women were not traveling alone but among others making the same journey. At the first rest stop—a well or spring where people could refresh themselves and animals could drink—we can see Naomi turning to her daughters-in-law for the final goodbye. The day was still young, and they had plenty of time to turn back, walking with others who had accompanied their friends and relatives for the first leg of their long trek westward.

With fervent emotion, however, both Ruth and Orpah professed their desire to continue with Naomi to Bethlehem. What a witness to Naomi's character and kindness! How her daughters-in-law must have respected, admired, and honored her. They adored her! They wanted to go with her, to be like her, to be the kind of woman she was.

Many of us are attracted to the spiritual life because of someone else's example. She's consistently joyful and optimistic, and we want that kind of inner peace. His preaching inspires and motivates us to delve more deeply into God's Word, and so we become faithful Bible readers. Her Bible studies open our eyes to what following Jesus really means, and we're eager to go.

Whether we're just starting out on our spiritual journey, or we're beginning the next leg of it, the first few steps are usually pleasant. Think of the three widows' first hour or so on the road. They were leaving their town behind, but they could still look back and see the outlines of familiar landmarks. The first stretch of road was not so isolated or untraveled that they felt frightened or disoriented. Accustomed to walking long distances, they weren't even especially tired. Yes, that's us when we're ready and willing to commit ourselves to go the whole way of discipleship with our Lord.

In your spiritual life, have you ever made a promise to Him you could not keep? Perhaps other things got in the way, or you just didn't realize how far from the familiar your commitment would bring you. You are not alone, for there's not a follower who has not stumbled, wandered away, or stopped by the side of the road. Let Him take your hand, lift you up, and guide you back. Let Him refresh you with His words of forgiveness and understanding. Begin again because each step draws you closer to Him.

Forgive me, dear Lord, for the times I have not fulfilled my promises to You and others. By myself I cannot follow, but with Your Spirit to help, guide, and support me, I can remain faithful to You. Grant me the gift of strength and perseverance to follow You! Amen.

Consider the Question

Naomi said, "Return home, my daughters. Why would you come with me? Am I going to have any more sons, who could become your husbands?"

RUTH 1:11 NIV

"W hat's in it for me?" is a natural question. If there's no material, spiritual, or emotional reward involved, why would anyone make this decision or continue along a particular path? When parting time came for the three women, Naomi urged her daughters-in-law to ask themselves, "What's in it for me?"

Naomi painted a bleak picture. Rather than suggest that the younger women would enjoy a fresh start filled with an array of possibilities in Bethlehem, she told the truth. She could promise nothing but hardship. As a widow with no more sons, Naomi, who was forced to rely on the charity of her relatives, had nothing to offer Ruth and Orpah, no matter how much she loved them.

What do you think following Jesus has to offer? Do you hear some say that His path leads to material gain, social success, and a problem-free existence? Are you attracted to Jesus Christ because someone assured you that He will shield you from the common trials and troubles of life? Those voices were not the voice of Naomi! Nor is it the voice of Jesus. When He said, "Follow Me" to His disciples during His earthly ministry, He offered no more than the opportunity to learn more about Him, go where He led them, and risk their lives for the privilege of sharing with others His message of love and salvation.

For those who followed Him then and for those who follow Him now, the same holds true. God may never ask you to suffer violent persecution on account of your faith or choose between life and death for His sake. But there will be choices to make and challenges to overcome. He may ask you to distance yourself from the friend who belittles your faith; the associate who uses derogatory, off-color language; the social group that scorns your obedience to God's commandments; the entertainment or friendship that would put you in spiritual harm's way.

What's in it for you, then? Why follow Him if He can't promise all the good things life has to offer? Challenge yourself with the question. Weigh the values of material striving versus spiritual strength, a relationship with the world versus a relationship with Him, a life of emptiness spent on yourself versus a life of meaning and purpose given for Him. Consider carefully before going any further!

Dear God, You have invited me to walk with You, and now I'm considering all that might lie ahead. Though You don't promise a smooth path the whole way, You do promise that Your presence, Your strength, and Your love will be with me throughout the journey ahead. Amen.

Come In

*"No, my daughters, return to your parents' homes, for I am
too old to marry again. And even if it were possible, and
I were to get married tonight and bear sons, then what?
Would you wait for them to grow up and refuse to marry
someone else? No, of course not, my daughters!"*

RUTH 1:12–13 NLT

*N*aomi's gentle humor would have made even the most resolute mind think twice. Her picture of Ruth and Orpah waiting until these two sons (born tonight!) reached marriageable age
must have made them smile. What's more, it gave them a graceful,
face-saving way out of their pledge to proceed to Bethlehem. "I see
what you mean," Naomi must have expected to hear. "You're right.
It's time for us to go back to our families and try to begin again."

While Naomi wanted the best for her beloved daughters-in-
law, could another motivation have been at play? Still reeling from
the loss of her sons, did she want to nurse her hurt alone for the rest
of her years? When we've lost what we've loved, it seems unfathomable we will ever love again. An emotional shell is our protection
against a world that has caused us so much pain. Yet as long as Ruth
and Orpah remained in the picture, Naomi could not avoid love.
They were actively loving, helping, supporting, and encouraging
her. When we don't want to believe in love, the last thing we want
is a constant reminder of love.

If you have ever wished you could pull the covers up over your head and shut the whole world out, then you know how Naomi may have felt. There are sorrows we believe no one else can understand, and we're right—they can't. But what they can understand is love. Though we carry a heavy burden, there are those who will help us bear it. We may feel God has abandoned us, but He is present. He's as close as the hands, heart, and voice of someone who is there, listening, caring, and walking right beside us.

Loss, when it touches your life, is agonizing. No, there's no way anyone in this world could possibly understand your heartbreak. But their presence, compassion, and willingness to be there with you are blessings that God has showered on you to help you through a difficult time. You have a burden, and they are there to carry it with you. You have a broken heart, and they are the healers God has sent to soothe the pain. "Go home!" That's what Naomi said to her God-sent helpers. What do you say?

---

*Lord God, so many times I've thought I could carry
my burdens alone. I didn't want anyone to know or
anyone to help. Thank You for those who have stayed,
who have seen through my shell. Thank You for those who
have heard in my "Go home!" Your "Come in." Amen.*

Cry for Hope

*"Life is harder for me than it is for you,
because the LORD has turned against me."*

RUTH 1:13 CEV

I n our heartache, many of us lash out against God. We wonder what we did that enraged God to the point that He would send such cruel punishment. Coming up with a reason or no reason at all, we conclude that God doesn't like us anymore and we can expect no more good from His hand. Naomi's misery had brought her to this point. She cried out in anguish, "God hates me!"

She felt she had a right to shake her fist at the heavens. Though her daughters-in-law had lost their husbands, just as she had, at least they still possessed their youth and could expect to remarry. Naomi was old and had no illusions about her prospects. Ruth and Orpah still could become mothers, but Naomi was well beyond the age of childbearing. They could return to their families sorrowful but without shame; Naomi would return to hers as a beggar, a charity case, and without hope for a better life.

Overwhelming stress, grief, or hardship can act like blinders. We're so focused on our emotions, feelings, and circumstances that they grow bigger than life, filling our entire line of vision so completely that we can see nothing else. Though we admit that others have their problems too, we're quick to point out the support, resources, or benefits they have that we do not. Even God couldn't make anything good out of our situation!

Yet God could, and He will. Give Him a try! When you're in the depths of sorrow, invite Him to come where you are. Share your grief with Him, and allow Him to lighten your burden, to give you hope. As He weeps with you, you will realize He isn't angry with you and isn't punishing you for anything you did. As He subdues your heartache, you will come to realize with calming certainty that He doesn't hate you—never has and never will. He loves you. In the comfort of His love, you place your trust.

As the blinders of grief gradually fall aside, your perspective widens, and for the first time in a long time you can see yourself and your situation more clearly. Even if you don't yet know what to do next, you're willing to wait on God to bring about His purpose for this season of your life. Remember, you're relying on the same God who brought Naomi out of her seemingly hopeless predicament! Trust Him because He will work blessings for you too.

Comfort me, heavenly Father, in my times of hopelessness.
When I can see nothing good, open my eyes to the
blessings around me, and enliven my imagination to
perceive the blessings You have in store for me. In all,
Lord, give me hope; let me trust in You. Amen.

Next Step

Again they cried openly. Orpah kissed her mother-in-law
good-bye; but Ruth embraced her and held on. Naomi said,
"Look, your sister-in-law is going back home to live
with her own people and gods; go with her."

RUTH 1:14–15 MSG

She just couldn't do it. As much as she adored her mother-in-law, Orpah began to realize all she would be leaving behind if she continued the journey. In Moab and among her own, she could go back to being the Orpah she had always been, while in Bethlehem she would need to learn new customs, make new friends, adopt new values and standards, and worship a new God, Naomi's God. Although the god of the Moabites, Chemosh, was feared as a dreadful, bloodthirsty deity, at least he was familiar to her. He's the god she grew up with. And who knows? It seemed to her that the almighty God of Israel let kind, devout Naomi down badly. Would Orpah risk the same treatment by pledging allegiance to Him? That was a risk she wasn't prepared to take. She had traveled this far, but now it was time to turn around.

No matter where we are on our spiritual path—just starting out or far along in commitment, maturity, and understanding—we pause along the way to evaluate where we're headed. Is spending time with God every day worthwhile, especially since we're so busy with other things? Does prayer make a difference? Should we open a conversation about Christ with an unbelieving friend? Should we invite a new neighbor to our church? How about the idea of increasing the amount of money we give—is it the most sensible thing to do, given the bills that stack up each month?

What we do next reveals who our god really is: an idol or the One True God. It's true that when we continue our journey with the God who loves us, we will leave certain things behind—things like trusting solely in our own judgment, always putting our own needs first, and stubbornly remaining in our spiritual comfort zone. Although we may come up with a list of excuses not to persist in our devotion to Him, the reality of His love is the reason we should.

Are you examining your faith life, wondering if you want to go ahead with Him? What is it He calls you to do? Maybe you have very sensible reasons why you are saying no. What are they? But rest assured that God has very wise reasons why He's inviting you to say yes.

When I discern that You are leading me to the next step, dear God, grant me the courage I need to say yes and then act on it. Although I'll be entering strange and unfamiliar territory, strengthen me with the knowledge that You are going right along with me. Amen.

Unconditional Commitment

Ruth said: "Entreat me not to leave you, or to turn
back from following after you; for wherever you go,
I will go; and wherever you lodge, I will lodge; your
people shall be my people, and your God, my God."

The poetic beauty of Ruth's response to her mother-in-law
touches hearts to this day. Her words continue to grace countless wedding ceremonies and still inspire pledges of deepest commitment, loyalty, and faithfulness between people. "I am coming
with you, my dear Naomi," Ruth's firm but gentle words say. "Let's
not talk about it any further because I've made up my mind."

Not just once but many times on our walk with Christ,
we'll find ourselves reaffirming our commitment to go where
He goes, stay where He stays, and embrace His people as
our own. Like Ruth, we don't know ahead of time precisely
where He will lead us. Ruth knew only that Naomi was taking
her to Bethlehem, but she had no certainty that they would get
there without difficulty. Where would they stay once they arrived?
Perhaps a hovel along with others as unfortunate as themselves; or
perhaps in the home of a wealthy relative who would take them
in. Though Ruth was ready to embrace Naomi's people, she had
no idea how willing they would be to embrace her. Israelites and

Moabites were longtime enemies. Despite all she didn't know, Ruth did know this: she would not turn back to her former home.

You are faced with similar uncertainties. God may bless your spiritual way with supportive friends, encouraging signs, and pleasant experiences; or He may bless you with a series of struggles, challenging obstacles, and difficult situations—yes, these are blessings too! He might invite you to stay among the rich or the poor, among the comfortable or the afflicted. God's people encompass believers of all abilities, races, ethnicities, social ranks, and economic levels. Who will He ask you to embrace? Who will be there to embrace you? You don't know.

Ruth's pledge of unconditional commitment came not from knowing what lay ahead but from knowing what lay within her heart. Pure love goes wherever the loved one leads, and Jesus, your eternal loved One, is leading you. Your complete faith in Him enables you to face whatever circumstances come your way, whether strange or familiar, difficult or comfortable. Your pledge of unconditional commitment starts with what you do know, and that's how deeply committed you are to traveling with the Lord your God.

My Lord and my God, let Your Spirit of love and devotion strengthen my commitment so I may speak the words of Ruth with my whole heart, mind, and soul. Let me trust You to take me where You will because it's there that I will find my true home. Amen.

Visible Faith

"Wherever you die, I will die, and there I will be buried.
May the LORD punish me severely if I allow
anything but death to separate us!"

RUTH 1:17 NLT

In Ruth's day, it wasn't unusual that an Israelite family would settle in a distant place. They were lured by business or trading opportunities or compelled to leave their home because of famine, pestilence, or warfare. Regardless of the reason they left, however, they intended to return so they could be buried among their own people. If an Israelite died abroad, often sons or other relatives were charged with taking their bones back to the land of Israel and interring their bones in the tombs of their ancestors.

Ruth's commitment to her new life went beyond the norm! She didn't want anything more to do with her old life, even in death. To seal her words, she swore an oath—not in the name of the Moabite deity, Chemosh, but in the name of the God of Israel. In this God she believed with her whole heart, and to this God she pledged her life and soul. She would serve Him for the rest of her days, inviting Almighty God to punish her if she failed to do so. And right now, on the road to Bethlehem, serving Him meant staying with Naomi.

Far from esoteric practices or mysterious rites, true service to our Father in heaven is open to all of us, visible to everyone around us, and completely down-to-earth. With her profession of faith, Ruth did not excuse herself from the world but became more directly and actively engaged with it. Rather than separate her from its necessities, her faith compelled her to join Naomi in her time of need. Ruth was willing to get her feet dirty along that dusty road, experience thirst and sore joints as they traveled, and stick with Naomi whether they ended up in a cave or a palace. Why? Because someone in her life was suffering, and that someone was Naomi.

The faith in your heart remains hidden from all but the eyes of God, but evidence of its presence is obvious to everyone around you. When you glimpse of God's gracious love for you, you can't help but respond with patience, compassion, and love for His other cherished children—your family members, friends, neighbors. As you experience the comfort of His forgiveness, you're compelled to forgive others. Enabled by His Spirit at work in your heart of faith, you can and you do. And that's faith that everyone can see.

Enable me, dear Lord Jesus, to make the faith You have planted in my heart real and visible. Open my eyes to the needs of others, and show me how I can ease their burdens in practical ways through Spirit-inspired words and actions of kindness, caring, and helpfulness. Amen.

Ruth-like Love

For now there are faith, hope, and love.
But of these three, the greatest is love.

1 Corinthians 13:13 CEV

ove, so easily expressed in words, proves itself over time. False love, based solely on feelings for a special person or enthusiasm for a particular project, is temporary. It won't hold up under the strain of changing circumstances or unexpected challenges. It shuns inconvenience, selflessness, and least of all, sacrifice. It ends where the real, unseen work, even unappreciated work begins. You probably can think of times when what you thought was love wasn't—when words of love did not lead to lasting love.

The Ruth-like love that God's Spirit plants and nurtures in our hearts grows deeper, stronger, and nobler with time. Fleeting feelings cannot diminish its commitment, and unforeseen events have no power to pull this love from its source and object, God. Ironically, struggle, hardship, and difficulties only make this love greater! Love that withstands obstacles is love tested and found true. This too you have seen in your life and in the lives of others.

If God has blessed you with genuine love for another person, you know that your love can overcome challenges, and only deepens as the years pass. If you are privileged to pursue the God-given love of special service to others, you know that this love withstands the often-laborious effort it takes to make a difference for the better in people's lives. If others honor you with their genuine love, you know that you possess something of divine worth.

Yet God's love for you goes beyond even the strongest, most fervent human love. It's there for you, even should you find yourself alone and left without the presence of others who can show their love for you. How do you know? Look inside you. The faith in your heart comes from the loving action of the Holy Spirit. Your ability to sense your weaknesses, confess your sins, and receive God's peace comes from the fact that Jesus first loved you, died for you, rose again, and lives to continue in His love for you. You can know love because God is love.

Look around you. See in the eyes of others their need for recognition, kindness, help, and encouragement—all things your Ruth-like love could fill through actions of love and compassion. And what Ruth didn't know yet about the love she promised Naomi on the road to Bethlehem is something you do know: when you put true love in action for others, it turns around to bless you even more!

God of love, thank You for making Your love known to me. Thank You, too, for the people in my life whose help, understanding, and kindness extend Your love to me. Grant me, I pray, the willingness to let Your love for me show in my love for others. Amen.

Lesson in Listening

*When Naomi realized that Ruth was determined
to go with her, she stopped urging her.*

RUTH 1:18 NIV

What can you say? When pure, God-planted love informs our words and actions, others find it hard, if not impossible, to bring a credible case against us. Even though those closest to us may not agree with what we're doing, or harbor personal misgivings about our decision, they finally must stand back and let love take its course.

That's the only thing Naomi could do after she had presented all her well-reasoned arguments to Ruth. Ruth listened to what Naomi said because she looked up to her mother-in-law and respected her opinion. As we'll see later in the story, Ruth wasn't a rash, stubborn, or headstrong woman; she obediently followed Naomi's directions to the letter in another situation.

No doubt Ruth thought through everything she heard and carefully considered each point. But she loved Naomi, she loved Naomi's God, and she was prepared to love Naomi's country and her people. Love won out, and Ruth made her decision: she was not returning to Moab, and she was not leaving Naomi. Naomi had no choice but to stop talking. Her daughter-in-law was going with her, with or without her permission.

As the two women rose with the other Bethlehem-bound travelers and continued on their way, the two women were silent, each lost in her own thoughts. We can see Naomi's shoulders slightly stooped, less with age than sorrow. We can imagine Ruth's face set with determination, her eyes straight ahead. The test of her newly professed love and the proof of her great commitment would come later.

Not everything that we have a mind to do is God-inspired. Sometimes even our best intentions and strongest yearnings stem not from God's call but from our own desires and imaginings. Most often, God uses the voices of those who love and care about us to advise us against a particular decision and to remind us of our real strengths, our more promising opportunities, our higher responsibilities, our wisest course of action.

Should you listen? Certainly. Listen like Ruth: carefully and respectfully. Pray for God's Spirit to give you the gift of discernment so you can test the validity of not just their reasons but your own. Search yourself for any motive, such as selfishness, self-interest, or self-aggrandizement, that could mask itself as true love or God's service. Let your words and actions, promises and commitments reflect His direction and unerring will for your life. Nothing else will fill your longings. Nothing else will bring you lasting joy.

Dear God, grant me the willingness to listen attentively and respectfully to the advice, reasons, warnings, and opinions of those who have my best interests at heart. Enable me to humbly accept and willingly follow Your direction for me, whether it comes from someone else or my own heart. Amen.

Traveling Companion

The two of them went on until they came to Bethlehem.

RUTH 1:19 ESV

If you have done any amount of traveling, you know that "getting there" isn't always hassle-free. While we dread a flat tire on the highway and face long lines and missed connections at the airport, Ruth and Naomi dealt with days of constant walking or donkey riding along bumpy, dusty roads. Then and now, travel can mean irregular meals, inadequate sleep, and long, monotonous hours of moving, waiting, and then moving again. Tempers run short, squabbles break out, and words are exchanged that, in normal circumstances, would never have crossed our lips.

For Naomi, this was a journey born of necessity. She was bereaved and despondent; she had nothing to look forward to but a deeply humiliating homecoming. Would she bring shame on the family, returning in her bereaved, helpless state? And what about the woman at her side—a Moabite, no less! The rigors of travel couldn't help but to have further darkened her already dark, angry outlook. Naomi could not have been a pleasant traveling companion.

How long did it take for Naomi's mood to affect Ruth's? Although younger than Naomi, she too became tired, thirsty, and achy. She too longed for a good meal and a long night in a clean, comfortable bed. Maybe they said little along the way, each woman lost in her own thoughts. Maybe they said too much and only later regretted their words and apologized to each other.

Spiritual travel can be no less rocky at times. We get tired of serving when we don't hear the thanks we feel we deserve. Rebuffs and setbacks make us wonder why we're trying so hard, especially when others seem to have it so easy. Our obedience to Christ brings no applause, and possibly ridicule or rejection from others, and we start complaining. And our Christian traveling companions? Sometimes they're the ones who are making the journey miserable with their constant squabbling, accusations, and criticisms!

But you know that the real joy is in getting there, and what happens on the road is all part of the story. The longer you travel, the more adept you become at avoiding road hazards and the better you're able to cope with life's physical and spiritual realities. Even more, your increasing experience brings you wider perspective, enabling you to help and encourage fellow travelers who aren't yet as sure-footed as God's Spirit has made you. On life's journey, He is giving you all you need to be a truly happy traveler—and traveling companion too.

Thank You, dear God, for putting me on the road to
spiritual maturity. As I discover joy in the journey,
enable me to comfort and befriend those who need me,
even if they aren't pleasant to be around. Grant me, Lord,
the privilege of being a good traveling companion. Amen.

What a Change!

When they arrived in Bethlehem the whole town was soon buzzing: "Is this really our Naomi? And after all this time!"

RUTH 1:19 MSG

ou haven't seen her since you both graduated from school. Now you run into her at your thirtieth class reunion, and you can't believe your eyes! From a shy, gawky teenager, she has become a poised, confident, professional woman. You greet her, eager to learn what has happened since you last saw her. You can't help but cheer her good fortune and admire her accomplishments.

But time isn't always kind. At the refreshment table, you notice a former star athlete, now frail with a debilitating illness. You hear someone call your name. The classmate who joined the military the day after graduation is coming toward you. Your heart sinks when you realize that an injury has left him a shadow of his former shelf. The intervening years have been cruel to many.

There was going to be a reunion in Bethlehem after the first to arrive spread the word that Naomi was not far behind. Friends, neighbors, and relatives were looking forward to seeing her again, inquiring about her health, and asking her what it was like in Moab. Were other women friendly? What kinds of food did they cook? How did they decorate their homes? And what was it like living among idol-worshipping Moabites? Their reputation for immorality and godlessness was well known.

Imagine the change in tone, the shocked faces, the exchanged glances when the women actually see Naomi. "She has aged," whispers one. "She keeps her eyes on the ground," says another. "She walks with a stoop well before her time," says yet another. This is not the woman they remembered at all. Naomi had left Bethlehem as the beloved wife of the good and honorable Elimelech and the mother of two fine sons. Instead of returning in triumph with several full carts of household goods and surrounded by husband, sons, daughters-in-law, and grandchildren, she quietly slips into town with nothing, leaning on the arm of a quiet Moabite woman. What a change!

When people you have not seen for years greet you, what do they see? Not on the outside, but on the inside? Are you kinder, gentler, and more understanding than you were ten, twenty, thirty years ago? Do you smile more, laugh more, and enjoy life more? Those are the changes that count, and they're the ones God desires to work in you. Whatever other changes time may bring, the changes His Spirit works in you are the ones worth celebrating.

Dear Lord God, send Your Spirit into my heart, mind, and soul! Let Him change me with His abundant gifts so that I will continue to grow in joy and peace, kindness and love, patience and understanding. Bring me the soul-deep beauty that only gets better with time, Lord. Amen.

Beloved Name

"Don't call me Naomi," she told them. "Call me Mara,
because the Almighty has made my life very bitter."

RUTH 1:20 NIV

ello! My name is _____ " the tag reads. Like everyone else attending the meeting, we fill in the blank, peel off the backing, and press the tag to our jackets. Now we can address one another by name. Yet we really don't know much about the person we've just met until we start making small talk and asking questions. It's only then that we discover where they work and what interests them. Only after chatting awhile do we get a glimpse into the other person's perspective and personality.

Among the Israelites of Bible times, however, the name itself would describe a person's appearance, personality, reputation, trade, or status in the community. For example, Naomi's name meant "pleasant," "lovely," "gracious." Her name tells us that, as a girl, she was congenial, attractive, graceful, and hospitable. With those qualities, she must have been a highly sought-after bride! What son's family wouldn't welcome a charming, well-mannered, and sensible young woman into the household? No doubt to the delight of Elimelech's parents, the not only lovely but devout Naomi became their daughter-in-law, and she presented them with two grandsons.

When Naomi returned to Bethlehem, however, there was no trace of the pretty young woman who had left only a decade ago.

Far from pleasantness, she exuded anger and resentment. Any hint of loveliness and graciousness had given way to the tight, gaunt grimace and raw defensiveness of the sorely disillusioned. Naomi? Her once-apt name had turned into a cruel joke. "From now on," we can imagine her spitting out to her former friends and neighbors who surrounded her, "my name is Mara!" Mara means "bitter." See the women shuffle uncomfortably. They try not to stare, but it's clear at first glance: life has turned very bitter for Naomi.

Although your given name doesn't necessarily refer to your personal attributes, God has given you a name that does. He calls you Beloved. Your name describes your relationship with Him through the faith that His Spirit nurtures in your heart. It celebrates the bond between you and your Brother Jesus Christ that He accomplished with His life, death, and resurrection. It proclaims your kinship with all believers of past, present, and future.

Beloved of God, the name He gives you means that you have in Him strength to lean on, wisdom to guide you, purpose to fulfill you, and forgiveness to bring you peace of mind. Think of yourself as lovely in His eyes because you are.

Thank You, heavenly Father, for the privilege of belonging to Your family. The name You have given me is a joy to repeat to myself, especially when I'm feeling discouraged or sad. Remind me who I am by whispering in my heart the name Beloved of God. Amen.

Empty or Full?

*"I went out full, and the LORD has
brought me home again empty."*

RUTH 1:21 NKJV

Where was Ruth all this time? While Naomi was pouring
out her woes to a spellbound audience, what was Ruth thinking? Despite the sublime outpouring of love she had expressed on
the road to Bethlehem—wherever you go, I will go!—she now sat
on the sidelines, silent and ignored. Even though she had sacrificed
her chances of remarriage and her own home in Moab for Naomi's
sake, her presence right now obviously meant little to Naomi. "I
have nothing, nothing at all!" Naomi declared.

When we're suffering a heavy loss, all we can think about is
what no longer belongs to us. It could be the loss of a loved one,
or our job, health, home, or financial security. In our truly painful
situation, we begin a narrative not of having lost something but
everything. Completely empty!

Yet our Lord is there, standing right beside us. We're not empty.
The old adage of seeing a glass half full or half empty applied to
Naomi, and it applies equally well to us. Although Naomi wasn't
returning to her extended family as a well-provided-for woman,
she had Ruth's love and presence, companionship and support.
She had someone to listen to her, sympathize with her, and help
with the daily necessities of life. She possessed a blessing that no
amount of money can buy, and that's the pure devotion of a loving

heart. Naomi was not empty at all, yet because she considered herself empty, she couldn't appreciate the glass half full she had before her. She could not say thank You to God for Ruth, His heart and hands at work in her life.

God fills your soul and your life with countless blessings, but in difficult times, it's hard to say thank You to Him. Mourning what you have lost, you're understandably not focused on where you are right now. Yet right here, right now is where God wants you to be. That's where He will fill your heart with the comfort of His presence and the promise of goodness to come. Right here, right now, He offers to lift the burden of worry from your mind and fill you with the knowledge that He is in control and with the hope that allows you to trust Him to take care of you in the days ahead.

You may not hear "thank you" from everyone whose life you touch with the blessing of your presence, help, and resources, but let God hear those words from you today. He will never leave you empty.

Dear God, thank You for the blessings I enjoy from Your hand each day. There are blessings I'm naming in my heart right now, and many more that I'm hardly even aware of. Fill me, Lord, with gratitude for Your gracious and ever-present love in my life! Amen.

God Caused This!

"Why would you call me Naomi? God certainly doesn't.
The Strong One ruined me."

RUTH 1:21 MSG

W hy did this happen to me?" We ask the question for a good reason when we're looking for what went wrong so we can put it right.

We can ask the question for a less laudable reason, however. We see that things aren't going the way they used to for us. We've lost our usual ability to make things go our way; what we once had, we have no more. From there we might decide, as Naomi did, that God caused our present misfortune. That's it! By putting all the blame on God, however, we're throwing away any chance of reaping blessings found only by those who are willing to receive them.

Yes, bad things (and good things) happen to believers and unbelievers alike. Though obedience to God's commandments and guidelines shields us from certain dangerous situations, we're not immune from the consequences of an imperfect world teeming with imperfect people. We can go from having it all to having nothing, just like anyone else. Yet there's a big difference when bad things happen to God's people, and it's that our security isn't in what we can do but in what He can do. We know He has the power to lift us up, and He will in His good time and at the right time.

Our misfortunes attune us to the sufferings of others. Through our suffering, we become more compassionate, more eager to help, more understanding when others find themselves in difficult places. We may find that what we had thought was a terrible setback begins a renewed and revitalized life, instills a fresh understanding of what's important, or provides exactly the experience we need to carry us through the years ahead. When our own hopes and dreams shatter, we're in a position to watch God put together a better future for us, one that beautifully conforms to His will, brings lasting joy, and fits us to fill our real purpose in life.

Sure, it's easy to believe, easy to feel joyful, when life is treating you well. But it's important to believe, hard to remain joyful, when you feel that everything's going against you. Let Him bless you with all He has to teach you when you're asking, "Why did this happen to me?" Those times test faith, and those are the times you want to remember that God is for you—in all ways, through all days, always.

Heavenly Father, in times of stress and difficulties,
fill my heart and mind with the words of Your promises,
the strength of Your presence, and the comfort of Your
love. When I can see no light in the darkness, grant me
the courage to walk with You to the light. Amen.

He Has Promised

God blesses those people who grieve.
They will find comfort!

Matthew 5:4 CEV

"I promise!" Seriously? It all depends on who's talking. From the lips of someone who has never before followed through on his promises, the words mean nothing. You might nod, smile, and think to yourself, *We'll see.* Yet when someone who has never before let you down says "I promise," you believe it.

In the Garden of Eden, God promised Adam and Eve that He would send a Savior who would redeem the world from the eternal consequences of sin. When? He didn't say; all He gave was His promise. Throughout the millennia, His faithful ones held on to God's promise because they saw Him keep promise after promise throughout their history. God promised Abraham a son, and Isaac was born; He promised to send relief to the Israelites held in Egypt, and Moses arose to lead them out; He promised to hear His people whenever they cried out, and He did. When they were hungry in the desert of Sinai, He sent manna and quail for them to eat. When they were thirsty, He showered them with water from a rock.

Naomi would have known these things. Overcome with despair, however, she couldn't imagine love ever again flowing from her stony heart or any good food—material or spiritual— ever again satisfying her hunger. Everything from now on would be bitter. It's as if she looked out the window, saw the darkness of night, and couldn't believe there would ever be a dawn.

In the depths of sorrow, we may feel that way. But we have God's promises! Just as Naomi knew how God had come through for His people up to her point in history, we have an even longer list of fulfilled promises to rely on, including God's promise to send a Savior. He said He would, and He did in the person of Jesus Christ, true God and true man. At precisely the right time, Jesus was born on earth. Just as the prophet Micah had predicted hundreds of years earlier, His birth took place in the tiny town of Bethlehem. Just as the psalmist predicted a thousand years before it happened, the Messiah was mocked, despised, and scorned by many, and He died a horrible death to atone for the guilt of sin. Promises fulfilled!

Today, God's promises to guide you, comfort you, forgive you, and strengthen you still stand. You can believe them because what He says goes. He has the will and the power to make it so. He promises!

Lord God, grant me the grace to put complete trust
in Your words of promise that I find in scripture.
Let nothing take me away from the security of knowing
You are always here for me and that Your help
will come exactly when I need it. Amen.

Together in Need

Encourage one another and build each other up,
just as in fact you are doing.

1 THESSALONIANS 5:11 NIV

fter the village women had heard Naomi's story again and again, and had shared their thoughts, opinions, advice, and judgments, it was time to get back to work. Water needed to be hauled from the well, bread kneaded once more before going into the oven, and berries, nuts, olives, and honey prepared for the evening supper. One by one, they scurried off; at last Naomi and Ruth were left by themselves. Where? We don't know. Maybe a compassionate innkeeper let them shelter temporarily in his courtyard, or a distant relative gave them a tiny room in his house. Perhaps they lodged in one of the caves around Bethlehem where sheep were kept, foreshadowing Jesus' birth so many years later!

Wherever the travelers found themselves, it was time for them to focus on the business of providing for their immediate future. You can imagine the two women sitting together and with heavy hearts, discussing their options. It's possible that in the quietness of this moment that Naomi came to realize how much Ruth's presence meant. Though the village women pitied Naomi, Ruth loved her. Though Naomi may not have cared what happened to herself, she cared what happened to Ruth. Ruth gave her a reason to think, pray, and plan.

Ruth had Naomi to thank for her initiation into the life

among the Israelites in Bethlehem. As stranger and foreigner, Ruth completely relied on Naomi's knowledge, kindness, and common sense for her well-being. Neither woman had an instant fix for the other's predicament, but they could face their challenges together.

We can't always change reality for others. We're powerless to remove illness, poverty, or workplace or relationship problems, but we can do what Naomi and Ruth did for each other. We can be there for our loved ones, letting them know that they aren't alone in their struggles. We can encourage them, point them to resources we may know about, and offer our insights and experience when asked. Most important of all, we can pray for them and with them. Where our power ends, God's begins, and He invites us to pray on behalf of others. What a privilege to lift a hurting soul to Him in prayer!

If there is someone in your life whose situation breaks your heart, pray for him or her. It's God's way of opening your eyes, and maybe the other person's eyes, to His presence and His power. Prayer will make a difference in that person's life, and in yours.

Hear my prayer, Lord God, on behalf of those I care about the most. Lift their burdens and heal their wounds, according to Your good will. Fill us with the certainty that You have compassion on all who suffer and Your love reaches to every heart and soul. Amen.

Spiritual Feast

He satisfies the longing soul, and the
hungry soul he fills with good things.

PSALM 107:9 ESV

In Bible times as today, there were women of wealth, power, and influence. Miriam, Moses' sister, proclaimed God's Word and led women in song, dance, and celebration. Deborah, God-fearing judge of Israel and courageous military leader, lived in the same era as Ruth and Naomi. Male clerics consulted with Huldah, God's prophet in Jerusalem. We remember that the godly woman of Proverbs 31 not only kept a comfortable home but made business decisions too!

When Mary and Joseph brought the infant Jesus to the temple in Jerusalem, the Holy Spirit inspired the prophet Anna's song of praise and adoration. During Jesus' ministry on earth, well-to-do women supported Him with their finances. In the early church, women were teachers, mentors, and evangelists.

Yet not all women had as many opportunities available. Local laws and social customs often created a nearly insurmountable barrier, making women dependent on men for their support. Ruth and Naomi found themselves in that situation. While Elimelech, Naomi's deceased husband, had owned property, Naomi could not inherit it; only her sons could, and they had both died. Elimelech's land would have been taken over by someone else, returning to Elimelech's family only if redeemed, or bought back from the present owner by the nearest male relative. Naomi would have to depend on him to give her the proceeds from the sale.

When Naomi and Ruth arrived in Bethlehem, however, their needs were pressing and immediate. They couldn't wait the months or years that it could take to locate a male relative willing to buy back the land, and trustworthy enough to turn over all the money received from the sale. They were hungry now.

For the spiritually hungry, it may appear that choices abound, but in fact they're limited to two. We can attempt to achieve a relationship with God through our personal effort and striving; or we can receive a relationship with God through Jesus' work on the cross. If we choose the do-it-myself method, we're always hungry to know if we have done enough to please God. We're starving for any new information or deeper understanding that might bring us closer to the reality of His presence. But if, by God's grace, we choose to let Jesus nourish us with His comfort, forgiveness, peace, and compassion, we have a feast right now. Even better, we need never worry about where the next meal is coming from! Come to His table and eat. He has prepared a banquet for you.

Relieve my spiritual hunger, Lord God, with the good food of the Gospel message Your life, death, and resurrection have brought to the world. Let my hunger be for nothing else than deeper faith in You, increasing confidence in Your love, and more perfect obedience to Your Word. Amen.

The Moabite

*So Naomi returned from Moab, accompanied by her
daughter-in-law Ruth, the young Moabite woman.*

RUTH 1:22 NLT

The Moabite. The inspired writer points out Ruth's ethnicity many times throughout the narrative. To his Israelite readers, Moabite stood for outsider; not one of us; idol-worshipper; of questionable character; enemy of Israel. They believed God's promise that the Messiah, descended from the line of the patriarch Abraham, would be born in their midst. So they drew the very human conclusion that no matter how devout or God-fearing a person of another nation might be, they couldn't possibly have a place in the Messiah's lineage. Prejudice, in the name of religious purity, was unquestioned.

Did God ever have a surprise for them! As we'll discover later in the story, God had a special role prepared for Ruth, the disparaged Moabite, a role that would place her soon as the great-grandmother of King David, a major figure in Israelite history and an ancestor of the Messiah, Jesus. Ruth the Moabite! A woman and an outsider.

To this day, God has a way of turning our prejudices inside out. Almost instinctively we dismiss certain groups of people or individuals as less important in God's kingdom or less deserving than ourselves of His love. But we're forgetting one salient fact: in God's eyes, we are all equally loved, equally His beloved children. While God has given us different talents, abilities, and resources, He excludes no one from His plans and purposes. Some have known Him and worshipped Him from our earliest years; others come to Him very late in life, even in their last moments on earth. Yet God's love is the same for all. There's no such thing as limited love when it comes to God.

God's great love knows no boundaries. No matter who you are or where you are—your past mistakes, your present situation, or your future potential—God loves you. He compares you to no one else, but sees only you, the you He longs to transform into His heart and hands in the world. And it might be a person you'd never expect that God sends to enrich your life with comfort, laughter, wisdom, or heart-deep affection and faithfulness!

If you feel the chill of prejudice, remember Ruth. Remind yourself that God loved her and put her name among the forerunners of Jesus Christ. Ask Him to forgive those who would treat you as anyone other than a fellow-redeemed child of God. Let no one relegate you to the spiritual sidelines. God may have a big surprise in store!

Dear God, grant me courage to stand up to prejudice
I may encounter in this life. Keep me, I pray, from any
prejudice I harbor in my thoughts or reveal in my words
and actions. Through the power of Your Spirit, help me
reflect Your love and compassion for all. Amen.

Hidden Beginnings

They arrived in Bethlehem at the
beginning of the barley harvest.
RUTH 1:22 MSG

I n March or April, Naomi and Ruth arrived in Bethlehem with no money, no place to stay, and no personal resources. They were completely dependent on others for the basic necessities of life. This is the lowest point of the narrative, but already there's a glimmer of hope. They arrived at the beginning of the barley harvest.

According to Israelite law, landowners were obliged to leave grain on the ground for the poor to pick up. They were never to send their harvesters back to clear the field of stalks they had missed. This worked in Naomi and Ruth's favor because it provided one way to get food without begging. They could put themselves among the poor of Bethlehem and gather enough grain to make a small loaf of bread for their dinner. So this is what it came to for the two formerly self-sufficient, self-respecting married women.

So often, what we see as the worst it can get sets up the foundation of blessings yet to come. For how many among us did it take years or decades of "doing our own thing" before we tried "God's thing"? How far did it take us to wander before we could appreciate the depth of His forgiveness and the breadth of His love? In the depths of loss, regret, and sorrow, new and better, God-blessed and bright beginnings take shape.

Like Naomi and Ruth, we can find ourselves forced to accept the only viable option available to us. With a sigh of resignation, we do whatever is necessary to provide for ourselves and those dependent on us. At the time, it felt as if all hope for a better life was no more than a pipe dream because there we were in that dead-end job; that small, cramped house; that dreary place.

Though picking up grain in the field during barley harvest may have seemed like the end of the line for Ruth and Naomi, it wasn't. It turned out to be exactly where God wanted them at that time. For them, that barley harvest was the God-blessed beginning of a beautiful story.

And the same is true for you. If you have been through a low time, count the blessings it has brought you. If you should ever face a difficult period of misfortune, keep your eyes open. What you think is the obvious end for you may be only the hidden beginning for God.

Dear God, open my heart and soul to what You might be putting in place today to equip my tomorrows with the skills, strength, and insight I need to better know You and serve the real needs of others. Grant me, I pray, the blessing of believing in new beginnings! Amen.

PART 2:

Ruth Meets Boaz

Family Connections

Naomi had a relative of her husband's, a worthy man
of the clan of Elimelech, whose name was Boaz.

RUTH 2:1 ESV

among the Israelites, the Law of Moses defined the structure of family and community life. A husband was responsible not only for his parents, wife, and children but also for the unmarried and widowed women among his extended family. Heads of families and clans had a religious duty to provide for their less-fortunate relatives and for the crippled, sick, and poor of their community. In observance of God's commandments to His people, house-holders were to provide hospitality to travelers—relatives, friends, and strangers alike. A prominent man in the community also was expected to spend his resources in defense of the village and its inhabitants. He was to redeem, that is deliver, his community from danger should it come under attack, and buy back anyone held captive by an enemy.

Of course, not all wealthy and powerful men fulfilled their obligations. Then as now, some chose to waste their bounty on personal gratification and wield power to their own advantage. Many men of means didn't take their responsibilities seriously, and others made careless, callous decisions. They didn't care what God had to say about "their" money and status. They would do as they pleased.

Boaz of Bethlehem, however, was not that kind of man. The

meaning of his name suggests "in him is strength," and Boaz lived up to his name. He was from a distinguished family and was a successful landowner with a reputation for wisdom, understanding, compassion, honesty, and trustworthiness. A devout and pious man, he ably and willingly fulfilled his God-given position in his family and community.

You too have a God-given position as family member, workplace associate, community resident, national citizen. These many connections nurture your social and emotional growth, and God uses them to feed your spiritual growth too. Without you being connected to others, and others connected to you, how would you ever know if you possess His spiritual gifts of patience, tolerance, faithfulness, and generosity? Your place in your family, workplace, community, and nation provides you with the opportunity to make God's presence, power, and love real in your life and in the lives of those around you.

How seriously do you take your place in your immediate family, in the larger family of your community, and in God's family of believers? How can you grow stronger in fulfilling the responsibilities of the position God has given to you?

Thank You, Lord, for the people around me.
In whatever way I'm connected to them, help me gladly
and willingly fulfill the position You have given me to the
very best of my ability. Thank You for the gift of others
who reach out to me with family love. Amen.

Our Kinsman-Redeemer

I am poor and needy; come quickly to me, O God.
You are my help and my deliverer; LORD, do not delay.

PSALM 70:5 NIV

With Boaz, we're introduced to the concept of a kinsman-redeemer. The kinsman-redeemer of an Israelite community was duty-bound to use his power, influence, status, and resources to do for others what they could not do for themselves. He was to provide leadership and protection, stability and safety so all in the village or town could lead peaceful and productive lives. As God's appointed representative, a kinsman-redeemer's personal qualities were to include obedience to God's commandments, moral cleanliness, and pure motivations and intentions in all his dealings.

Boaz, as kinsman-redeemer, foreshadowed Jesus' earthly ministry and the purpose of His birth into the world. Perfectly fulfilling His God-appointed role as our kinsman-redeemer, Jesus used His divine power to do for people what they could not do for themselves. He healed physical infirmities and satisfied physical hunger during His ministry so those who followed Him then and those who follow Him now could understand His ability to heal spiritual infirmities and satisfy spiritual hunger.

Jesus became our kinsman by assuming our humanity, and He became our redeemer by giving Himself to deliver us from the bondage of sin. Though guilt would hold us captive, He bought us back, not with money or military might but with the selfless and effective gift of His life. It was all part of His Father's plan of salvation from the beginning, and Jesus, true God and true man, didn't flinch in fulfilling it. His resurrection from the dead proved His was not a self-indulgent martyrdom but the outcome of a God-appointed role taken on out of boundless, unconditional love.

You are a member of God's family through faith in Jesus' sacrifice for you. He is your kinsman-redeemer, ready and able to forgive your offenses, resolve your guilt, comfort your heart, and bring you peace of mind. This is something you cannot do for yourself—no one can, except your Savior, Jesus.

If there has been someone in your life who has rescued you from a dangerous situation, you have a glimpse of what a kinsman-redeemer does. If you have ever filled that role for someone else, or you have witnessed a life-saving moment in person or through the media, you can get an idea of the difference a deliverer makes. Consider how Jesus is your kinsman-redeemer, your deliverer, from spiritual death. It's all because of your Spirit-given relationship with Him!

Lord Jesus, help me grow in understanding and appreciation of what You have done for me as my divine kinsman-redeemer. Awaken the eyes of my spirit to the truth of Your life, death, and resurrection so faith, firm and steadfast, will keep me forever in Your family of believers. Amen.

Unspoken Needs

Ruth the Moabitess said to Naomi, "Please let me go to the field, and glean heads of grain after him in whose sight I may find favor." And she said to her, "Go, my daughter."

RUTH 2:2 NKJV

The Law of Moses dictated that harvesters were not to pick fields clean, but allow the poor to glean grains that had fallen. This is the task Ruth offered to take on. She did not ask Naomi to go with her, nor did she wait for her mother-in-law to volunteer. Here is a telling example of Ruth's thoughtfulness and selflessness.

Even if Naomi possessed the stamina a long day of outdoor labor required, think how humiliating it would have been for her to glean. Her neighbors had seen her leave Bethlehem as a respected married woman and mother, and now they would watch her, stooped and sweaty, working in the fields among the impoverished. Ruth, knowing her mother-in-law's dark state of mind, may have felt that adding another burden would only deepen her depression. And who knows? Maybe the undeniable fact that Ruth was willing to pick up grain in a field so they could eat would jar Naomi into realizing the worth of Ruth's presence. From Naomi's simple assent, we know that she was relieved.

"The friends who really help," someone once remarked, "aren't those who do what you ask them to do, but do before they're asked." Those are the friends who understand how it must feel to be in your situation. They ask themselves what they would want someone to do for them under similar circumstances, and they go ahead and do it. Their kindness isn't simply an appreciated action stemming from a stated request but a blessed response to an unspoken need. Encouraging words; moral support; a friendly visit; a patient listener. Would you ask someone for these things? Probably not. But there are times you yearn for someone to care, and you'll never forget the friend who hears what you didn't say.

Naomi heard what Ruth didn't say when the Moabite entered her home as a bride. Added to any young woman's fears and uncertainties, Ruth was joining a family whose customs and traditions differed from those she grew up with. Young Ruth would not have asked for any special help, but Naomi obviously provided it with kindness, gentleness, and love.

Do you listen for hidden needs? When you do, you hear what words cannot express. Are you the kind of friend who doesn't need to be asked? When you are, you have let someone know you truly understand.

Dear God, open the ears of my heart to hear the needs
of those I love; open the eyes of my heart so I can respond
in the way I would want them to respond to me.
Enable me to be the one who shows I really care. Amen.

Dignity Within

Ruth went out to gather grain behind the harvesters.

RUTH 2:3 NLT

*P*icture what it must have been like for Ruth as she set out for
a field. There was a slight chill to the air in that early-morning
hour, but she knew the afternoon would bring hours of penetrating heat. Walking the dusty path that led to the fields, several careworn, stooped women were slowly making their way in the same
direction. No one spoke, leaving each to ponder the circumstances
that had brought them this low.

Was Ruth thinking back to her family in Moab? If she had
gone back to her mother's house, she would be sitting among
friends, eating bread, biting into fruit, savoring stews, and drinking tea. Maybe someone would know of a man who would be
interested in marrying her. She could be a wife again, maybe even
a mother. She would have dignity and respect in her community.
She wondered if Orpah had received inquiries yet. Why shouldn't
she? Her sister-in-law was still young, healthy, and attractive. Ruth
pictured Orpah a year from now beaming with pride, a robust
newborn son cradled in her arms.

But Ruth dismissed such thoughts because they dragged her
down. She had made her decision, and this was the reality of her
present situation. She was among the lowest of the low in Bethlehem, her new home. Even servant girls ranked higher than she!
Though her better-off neighbors didn't even attempt to hide their

disdain for harvest-pickers, Ruth walked deliberately and with as much dignity as she could muster out to a landowner's field.

Even today, certain work is looked down upon. Those who occupy these positions are often treated with disdain. If you are or have been in a low-status job, you know how it feels. Yet there's a blessing to harvest, and that's the knowledge that true dignity comes from inside, not outside. Your worth as a human being, a woman beloved of God, is no less if you are the lowest ranked person, and no more if you are the highest. You can walk with confidence, take pride in a job well done, and share with others the joy you possess in Christ. As someone who cares, you can make it a point to acknowledge and thank every person whose work serves you and those you love.

Thank your heavenly Father for where you are now. If you feel you have "come down" in the world, let Him lift you up. Let His Spirit flood your heart with the divine dignity that no person, place, or circumstance can take away from you.

Loving God, fill my heart with confidence, self-respect,
and dignity so I may fully embrace the circumstances
I'm in today. Grant me acceptance where necessary and
the vision to make changes for the better where I can.
In every place, I know that You are present. Amen.

As It Happened

As it happened, she found herself working in a field that belonged to Boaz, the relative of her father-in-law, Elimelech.

RUTH 2:3 NLT

*a*s it happened." Chance? Coincidence? Good luck? Or God's hand in the lives of those who love Him? You decide.

Naomi's husband, Elimelech, had been a landowner. In all likelihood, he had sold the land to someone else before leaving Bethlehem, intending to buy it back upon his return for his sons to inherit. But the three men's deaths dashed those plans. As a woman, Naomi could not buy back the land. She needed to find her nearest male relative willing to do it for her as her kinsman-redeemer. At any rate, Elimelech's fields were ripe for harvest, and the present owner was entitled to the proceeds from what he had planted.

Naomi and Ruth needed food today, and neither woman wanted to beg. Ruth's willingness to take on the only work open to her was an act of humble obedience to the reality of her situation. And it's this humble obedience that put her at the right place at the right time. If you had asked her why she chose this particular field to enter, she might have replied, "It was the first one I came to," or "I followed some other women, and that's where they went." If you could have asked God, you would have heard a different answer.

From our point of view, many of our choices are simply a matter of practicality or necessity. Like Ruth, we go about our daily responsibilities, and we attach no spiritual significance to our actions. But God, who knows our present and our future, has the better view. There are times when He directs our path through those things called "chance" or "coincidence" so we will go where He wants us to go, meet who He wants us to meet, be where He wants us to be at exactly the right time.

Your love for Him prompts your obedience to Him and your commitment to His principles of hope, humility, and faithfulness. These are the things God uses to work His will in the world. Your decisions based on obedience to God might not seem momentous. If you had asked Ruth, she was only doing what she had to do to put food on the table that night. "As it happened," she walked into a field belonging to Boaz.

How many "as it happened" instances have taken place in your life? Chance? Coincidence? Good luck? Or God's hand in the life of someone who wants to follow Him?

Thank You, dear Jesus, for the "as it happened" events in my life. I may not have seen Your will at work then, but I do now. Despite myself, I found myself at exactly the right place at the right time. Let me forever remember that You direct my path! Amen.

Words Matter

*While she was there, Boaz arrived from Bethlehem and
greeted the harvesters. "The LORD be with you!" he said.
"The LORD bless you!" the harvesters replied.*

RUTH 2:4 NLT

Words matter! Look at the words Boaz used as he entered his field. As the landowner—the boss, the man in the corner office—he might have thought himself entitled to put on a few airs, display a little pomp befitting his position, speak condescendingly to those beneath him. But Boaz did no such thing. His civil, courteous greeting set the tone of the relationship between manager and staff. His words elicited a similarly polite greeting in return and showed that Boaz was a humble, caring man who respected those under his authority, and they respected him.

The words we use reflect how we think about ourselves, our outlook on life, and how highly we regard those around us. Believing that God loves us, we have every reason to love ourselves. Our God-centered self-worth creates positive thoughts and self-talk. Our outlook brightens when we love who we are, and when we love who we are, we're able to love others too. And where there's God-given love, there are words of genuine caring, respect, and understanding.

The more we refuse to harbor anger, envy, regret, and resentment, the fewer destructive words will enter our conversations. The longer we practice godly attributes of faithfulness, humility, honesty, and love for others, the less often it will even occur to us to utter a coarse word or make a mean-spirited comment. We don't have to worry about something "slipping out" of our mouths when it isn't in our hearts in the first place!

Your words matter to you and to those around you. Love yourself because God loves you, and He doesn't make mistakes when He loves. Think well of yourself, and speak well of yourself. Love others because God loves them. Think the best of them, and speak well of everyone as far as the truth allows. The positive things you say can turn an atmosphere of suspicion and wariness to one of civility and well-being.

If you want to change your words, first change your thoughts. Ask God to guide your eyes to see the best in yourself, in others, and in your present circumstances. If you're in a position of authority, your words set the tone of your home, your workplace. They dictate how others will respond to you. If you are among others in any way, your words can create new, positive, and productive relationships. Your words matter.

Holy Spirit, fill my heart with the kind of thoughts that
bring about kindly, respectful, loving, and gentle words.
Grant me the privilege of being the one who uplifts,
encourages, and inspires others through the words I use and
the things I say. Put in my mouth words of peace. Amen.

Risky Business

*"Take the thousand and give it to the one who risked the most.
And get rid of this 'play-it-safe' who won't go out on a limb."*

MATTHEW 25:28–29 MSG

*G*iving is risky business. For instance, consider the way Boaz treated those under him. He respected them, without waiting to see whether they would respect him in return. While giving, he risked that some would not behave in a respectable way; and as we'll discover later in the story, not all of them did. But their conduct did not stop Boaz from being who he was, a man who respected others.

Loving others is another example of risky giving. Most of us have, at some time, extended love to someone else, only to have it dismissed or unappreciated. Yet to stop loving would render all relationships impossible. It's the same with an act of compassion. We risk being taken advantage of, but to stop doing what we can to lift the suffering of others would turn our hearts to stone. We're willing to risk being compassionate because human empathy prompts it, our obedience to God demands it, and our Spirit-inspired faith compels it.

Our risk-taking God surrounds all of us with the wonder and beauty of His creation, even though not everyone thanks Him. He provides blessings to all without waiting to make sure each one of us will realize that everything we have comes from His hands. He loves us so completely that He was willing to send His Son into the world to bring us close to Him. Does everyone care? Does everyone love in return? Sadly, no. Yet there's no way God is going to stop being who He is—our heavenly Father, our compassionate Friend, our ever-present Counselor and Peace.

With the power of His Spirit strengthening your faith and motivating your words and actions, you can take risks. You can risk sharing a proportion of your time, abilities, and income to help others because you trust that God will see to your needs in the future just as He always has and continues to do today. You can risk extending a warm welcome to visitors and newcomers because you never know who may become a loving, supportive friend. You can risk giving, and giving generously, because that's the kind of person you are.

Ironically, it's in giving that you receive life's blessings in abundance. With Spirit-filled giving come fulfillment and contentment, meaning and purpose, self-worth and personal dignity. When we're in the business of risky giving, we have the joy of giving our best—just as Jesus did for us.

Dear Lord Jesus, increase my willingness to risk giving to others without waiting for others to give to me first. Enrich my life with the joy of sharing what You have given me with those who have less because I know that You will always take care of me. Amen.

A Question of Caring

*Boaz said to his young man who was in charge of
the reapers, "Whose young woman is this?"*

RUTH 2:5 ESV

It was harvesttime, and landowners' profits hinged on how thoroughly, quickly, and efficiently workers could get the crops in. Most overseers would not have bothered to look twice at an individual harvester as long as he was working, and they certainly wouldn't have so much as noticed who was picking up fallen grain (unless the overseer thought the harvesters were leaving more grain on the ground than he was willing to give to the poor). For sure, Boaz cared about the harvest because he was a good and careful manager; but he cared about people more. When he saw someone he didn't recognize, even among the non-profit-producing gleaners, he wanted to know who it was.

As we go about the many responsibilities of our day, often we hardly notice the new face among us. It's not that we don't care about other people because we believe we do; it's just that we're so focused on our tasks that we forget there are those around us who long to be seen and recognized and their presence acknowledged. Perhaps it's someone we frequently see but have never bothered to get to know, or the next person standing in the checkout line, or the newcomer who's too shy to say the first hello.

Boaz asked, "Who is she who's come to glean this morning?" so he could find out about this stranger who had obviously fallen on hard times. Boaz may have helped other needy Bethlehem families, and he wanted to know if another household was in need of his help. Today, we can ask, "What's your name?" "Where are you from?" "How can I help you?" When we care about people—friend, family, visitor, stranger—we ask questions. We want to know who has come to our attention, especially those we can see are in need.

In a world that all too happily measures value in terms of production and possessions, God invites us to find value in people. God's Spirit enables our eyes to look beyond our paycheck, our goods, and our security to see those who have no paycheck, goods, or security. Who are they? What do they lack that we can provide? He releases our hearts from the captivity of things we have and opens us to the condition of people.

Who belongs to those, the sad, despairing, troubled, sorrowful faces? How can you bless their days? You'll never know until your questions show you care.

When I am blind to the needs of others, Lord, open my eyes to their plight, and make me willing to find out who they are and how I can help. Maybe it's just a warm smile from someone who cares; maybe more. Grant me the joy of asking. Amen.

A Different Attitude

The overseer replied, "She is the Moabite who came back from
Moab with Naomi. She said, 'Please let me glean and
gather among the sheaves behind the harvesters.' "

RUTH 2:6–7 NIV

Ruth presented herself to the overseer of the harvest field. She didn't need to ask permission to gather leftover grain because that was her right both as a widow and an alien. Nonetheless, her sense of propriety, gratitude, and respect for the property of others prompted her to introduce herself to the person in charge before she began her work.

How differently events would have unfolded if Ruth had walked into that field with a defensive attitude! If, out of shame and embarrassment, she had hidden her face and tried to stay outside anyone's notice, the foreman would have said to Boaz, "I have no idea who she is." If bitterness or hostility had made her words sharp, angry, and rude, the foreman would have advised Boaz to keep his distance. A bad attitude on Ruth's part would have completely changed how others responded to her and substantially altered subsequent events.

In our own lives, a Spirit-fed, Spirit-led attitude makes a difference. Our confidence in God's presence shields us from defensiveness, and our trust that God will work things out keeps us from despair and hopelessness. Our willingness to forgive protects us from hate, bitterness, and vengeful imaginings; our certainty in

God's love for us endows us with dignity, whatever our situation, and enables us to treat others with genuine humility and respect. We realize that an attitude problem doesn't stem from our circumstances but from our broken relationship with God.

God promises certain spiritual gifts to those who place their trust in Him. They include many of those Ruth exhibited in her words and actions that morning in the field of Boaz. She had no need to hide, for she was God's beloved daughter. She wasn't angry or bitter because where she was, God was present. She didn't fight her fate or blame others for it but did what was in her power to change things for the better.

Your faith in Him opens you to a Ruth-like attitude. His Spirit empowers you to face reality with acceptance of what you cannot change at this time, and strengthens you to take whatever productive steps you can, difficult or unpleasant as they may be to you. With His Spirit in the lead, rest assured that you are where you need to be for His plans and purposes to take place in your life.

When my attitude gets in the way, Lord God, forgive me.
Let me invite Your Spirit into my heart to strengthen my
relationship with You, receive Your spiritual gifts, and then
embrace myself, my circumstances, and those around me with an
attitude of thankfulness and humility, dignity and grace. Amen.

An Assertive Woman

Be strong in the Lord and in the power of His might.

EPHESIANS 6:10 NKJV

*a*s a person in poverty, Ruth was entitled to glean but no more. Gathering left-behind sheaves, however, would have been the task of household servants for their use or for storage. Ruth may not have understood the difference when Naomi explained to her the intricacies of Mosaic Law. Or it's possible that in addition to being a humble and respectful woman, she also was an assertive woman. *What's the harm in asking?* she might have thought. After all, the worst she could get for her question would be a decisive no for an answer and a sharp reminder that she had to keep to her place.

So often, we equate humility and respect with timidity and fearfulness. Many of us think that being assertive means behaving aggressively and belligerently to get what we want, so we avoid asserting ourselves. In a well-intentioned desire to nurture godly qualities, we act like buoys bobbing in whatever direction the wind sends us! But God's Spirit at work in our heart does not compel us to put our lives in the hands of others and accept whatever they decide to give us and however they choose to treat us. Far from it, for among the many godly qualities the Spirit works in us is boldness.

God-given boldness empowers us to claim what is rightfully ours and invites us to ask for what would enhance our well-being and the well-being of others. Godly boldness gives us poise and grace to respond appropriately to the response we receive, whether yes or no. We rely on God's wisdom to show us where we ought to let the matter drop and where we need to assert ourselves more forcefully.

Yet boldness without humility quickly morphs into arrogance, and we hear ourselves demanding that others give us what we want and do what we say. Boldness without respect for others leads us to put ourselves ahead, without a thought for those we're pushing aside. That's why God-given boldness doesn't come alone but with other gifts, such as humility, gentleness, and kindness.

Are there situations in which you need God-given boldness? Are you so intimidated by certain people that you find it difficult, if not impossible, to speak your own mind? Look within yourself for your Spirit-inspired boldness, born of God-pleasing humility. This is the kind of boldness that allows you to assert yourself in the best ways and for the best reasons. In you, as in Ruth, Spirit-fed boldness is in perfect harmony with a Spirit-led life!

Holy Spirit, grant me the boldness I need to stand up for myself and others when the situation calls for it. Help me assert myself with a humble attitude and through reasonable requests; with respectful words and through appropriate actions. Let what I say and do bring glory to You. Amen.

Unacceptable Behavior

"She came into the field and has remained here from morning till now, except for a short rest in the shelter."

Ruth 2:7 NIV

Sexual harassment may have been the reason for Ruth's "short rest in the shelter." Rude gestures, insulting propositions, and ethnic slurs (Everyone had heard about the morals of Moabites!) had reduced her to tears!

Translators have grappled with the meaning of the Hebrew phrases, which are disconnected and laced with pauses, suggesting that the overseer was upset or embarrassed. He knew that Boaz, a man of good character, would not want to hear what he had to say; but the truth compelled him to report what he knew had happened. As we'll see, Boaz's response makes sense only if the male field hands had been behaving badly.

While the offensive behavior of others waylaid Ruth for a short time, she quickly composed herself. Naomi was at home, depending on her to bring back grain so she could bake bread for their meal. Although she may have been willing to go hungry just to get away from their leering looks, she couldn't let Naomi down. So Ruth swallowed her pride and returned to the field.

To this day, many women are subjected to sexual harassment in their workplaces or communities, coping with everything from "harmless" teasing to physical assault. Like Ruth, not every woman can leave her job or report the matter to management without serious consequences, so they bear with it as best they can. If you have ever been in a similar situation, or know someone who has, you understand Ruth's position. Sometimes, for the well-being of those you love, there is nothing you can do but press on.

When you find yourself in a predicament with nowhere to turn, your Heavenly Father invites you to turn to Him in prayer. You might ask, "What good would prayer do in my case?" Yet prayer indeed changes things. Prayer—time alone with God—offers comfort for your aching heart. You can confide in Him everything that is happening. Everything, even if you have trouble finding the words to describe your hurt, anger, and embarrassment. Prayer—a heart crying out to God in the middle of a trying day—brings the force of His presence to your mind. Prayer is your determination to do what you must do for the sake of yourself and others and leave the rest in His hands. He sees what you see, hears what you hear, and knows what you know about what's taking place. Put the matter in His hands. Receive His strength.

Lord God, thank You for being with me every moment,
especially those times when I'm hurt, offended, or insulted
by the behavior of others. Show me how to act, what to say,
what to do; most of all, teach me to forgive because only
forgiveness will heal my broken heart. Amen.

Gracious Invitation

*Boaz said to Ruth, "Now, listen, my daughter, do not go
to glean in another field or leave this one, but keep close
to my young women. Let your eyes be on the field
that they are reaping, and go after them."*

RUTH 2:8–9 ESV

Did the foreman see Ruth, shamed and indignant, head for the
road, only to turn around again? Had someone told him that
Ruth intended to glean someplace else tomorrow? What happens
next makes either scenario likely.

Boaz, among the highest-ranking men in Bethlehem, walked
directly over to Ruth, the lowest. From his foreman, Boaz had
just learned how she had fallen from protected wife to vulnerable
widow, and he realized that she was not experienced in the ways
of the world. So Boaz advised her not to leave his property for
another. He was well aware that his land-owning neighbors and
their overseers turned a blind eye to what went on among field
hands, harvesters, and gleaners. In addition, he invited her to join
the female servants of his household, where she would find safety
in numbers.

A kinsman-redeemer's duty was to protect those dependent
on him, and this is what Boaz did for Ruth. He fulfilled his obligations honorably and conscientiously. This stranger was not a
member of his household, yet he invited her in because he saw

her defenselessness. She was weak and helpless, he had compassion on her plight, and he had the power to help her. His compassion reflects the great compassion God has for all who are weak, helpless, and bereft of protection. Doesn't that include all of us? Who among us is so strong, powerful, secure, and invincible that they do not need God, our divine Kinsman-Redeemer?

God saw that we would never have the power to protect ourselves against sin, so He came to us in the person of Jesus Christ to walk with us and guide us along the best and safest paths. He knew that, left on our own, we could not work our way into His family, so He sent His Holy Spirit to invite us in and make us one of His own. Yet how many among us resist the blessings God desires to shower on us? How many of us leave for other fields, thinking we'll be happier, safer, more satisfied elsewhere?

You will find that Boaz's words to Ruth reassured her. As your Kinsman-Redeemer, let God's words to you in scripture do the same. Listen for His counsel, breathe in His comfort, stay in His household, and receive the peace, strength, and assurance that only He can give.

Thank You, dear God, for coming to me where I am and inviting me into Your family of believers. Protect me with Your strength and power, and let Your gracious words bring me the confidence and assurance I need to continue despite difficulties, and persevere despite hardship. Amen.

A Way Through

*O LORD my God, in You I put my trust; save me
from all those who persecute me; and deliver me.*

PSALM 7:1 NKJV

*a*s her kinsman-redeemer, Boaz made arrangements to ensure
Ruth's safety. Notice that he didn't help Ruth by handing her
a purse full of money and sending her on her way. He could have,
but he didn't. Instead, he gave her a way to do her work without
being subjected to unnecessary fear or distraction. Again, Boaz's
response to Ruth's plight mirrors God's actions in our lives today.

Yes, God has the power to instantly solve our problems,
whether they're financial, emotional, or physical. With a mere
word from His mouth, He could relieve us of our burdens and set
us up on Easy Street for the rest of our lives. But He doesn't. His
compassion toward us, like Boaz's compassion toward Ruth, offers
help and protection as we fulfill our responsibilities of the moment
and face our current challenges. God doesn't wrench control from
our hands but strengthens our hands. Rather than disable us by
arbitrarily changing our reality, He enables us to infuse our reality
with courage, wisdom, compassion, and love.

In every situation, you have recourse to prayer. You can tell Him
what you fear, what you find unbearable, and what you feel you
just can't handle, and rest assured that He has heard you. Though
you don't know how He will act on your behalf, you know that He
will act. Perhaps you'll experience a sense of renewed commitment

and increased courage within yourself, giving you the confidence you need to continue. Perhaps you'll notice changes taking place that make it easier for you to cope. Wait and see!

You have His Word, the Bible. His active Word in your heart and mind works in you deeper faith, protection from hopelessness, and increased knowledge of His work among people. You may even find yourself thanking Him for *not* taking away the difficulties that you have gone through in the past, because without them there's so much you would never know. You learned things you could have learned in no other way. And just as He gave you the wisdom, courage, know-how, and perseverance to overcome hardship in the past, He will do so again today.

Allow God to protect you, to make your way smoother, according to His good will. You have your Kinsman-Redeemer in Him, the one who can transform the worst of burdens into the best of blessings.

Redeemer and Lord, thank You for granting me the joy
of working through my problems and overcoming hardships
surrounded by Your protection, enabled by Your power,
and led by Your guidance and wisdom. Remove my fear of life's
burdens because I have all the strength I need in You. Amen.

God's Rules

*"I have warned the men not to bother you, and whenever you are
thirsty, you can drink from the water jars they have filled."*

RUTH 2:9 CEV

*B*oaz exemplified respect and kindness in his dealings with others but not permissiveness. While compassion compelled him to grant Ruth special privileges, justice bound him to confront wrongdoers with firmness and decisiveness. In no uncertain terms, he ordered the men who had been harassing Ruth to stop immediately. Their behavior was neither okay nor acceptable. It would not be—could not be—overlooked if everyone in his field were to work safely and productively.

Boaz's rules for his workers are like God's commandments for believers. God set His law in place so we would know what's expected of us, how we are to worship Him, and how we are to treat others. When we behave in ways contrary to His law, God's reprimand comes in the form of a burdened conscience, a guilty heart, a ruptured relationship with our Lord and Savior. By these things we know that what we thought, said, or did was not right in God's eyes; it caused offense to someone else; it proved a distraction to our growth in godly and God-pleasing qualities; and it could turn others to the same sin if we're allowed to persist in sin seemingly unscathed and unaffected. At the foundation of God's justice is God's love for us and for everyone else in His family of believers.

Guilt feelings aren't pleasant, and some people try to ignore them or dismiss them with excuses, assuring themselves that what they did was okay, given the circumstances. But when God says no, He's saying it to guide our growth in faith and goodness. When we live by His rules, we work more productively—and joyfully—in His field and among others.

Listen when His Spirit uses your conscience, your better knowledge, or unhappy consequences to admonish you. It's what reminds you of God's commandments and His will for your thoughts, words, and actions. Allow His Spirit to guide your humble confession before your heavenly Father, sharing with Him everything that troubles your heart. There's no sin so big that He won't forgive it, and no sin so small that it couldn't disturb your peace of mind and disrupt your relationship with Him.

With His forgiveness comes healing. With His grace comes His promise to help you change what needs to be changed in your life. He will reprimand you because He is gracious and just, and He loves you.

Dear Lord, thank You for the privilege of hearing Your words of admonition when I have done wrong. Help me never shrink from the demands of Your commandments, but rely more fully on You for the strength, power, perseverance, and wisdom to follow Your will and guidance. Amen.

Love Unlimited

She dropped to her knees, then bowed her face to the ground.
"How does this happen that you should pick me out
and treat me so kindly—me, a foreigner?"

RUTH 2:10 MSG

Ruth showed her deep gratitude in the style of her time—on bended knees, her face to the ground. As a non-Israelite, she would have expected discrimination, if not persecution, in her new home. Yet not only had Boaz noticed and protected her, but he also offered her the privilege of joining other women under his care. She was thankful but shocked. Did Boaz realize that she was not an Israelite? What did she do to deserve his compassion? Is this too good to be true?

Her very human reaction to her good fortune is similar to ours as we begin to understand what God has done for us. We say, "Thank You, God," but at the same time doubt that He knows all the ways we have fallen short of worthiness. We say, "Thank You, God," yet hold His forgiveness at arm's length, knowing we don't deserve it, and concocting ways we could perhaps earn it. We say, "Thank You, God," and then wonder if His kindness, His compassion, and His love for us are all too good to be true.

Yes, too good to be true if you look at yourself. But look at God! God is love, and He loves because that is the God He is. He has promised to love you, and He will love you, even if you imagine yourself unlovable. He takes you into His household, even if you are a stranger to those around you. He invites you to drink from the same well of living water provided for all His daughters and sons.

There's no way you can earn what God has ready to give, any more than Ruth could somehow earn the blessings that Boaz extended to her that day. What sense would it have made for her to say, "Oh, no, thank you, Boaz; I'll wait until I've earned these blessings"? But there is no way Ruth could have earned them. Your soul longs for His comfort today; why wait for some future time when you will be no closer to earning it than you are right now?

Ruth's astonishment, like yours, is natural when confronted with such overwhelming kindness. Because this is coming from your Heavenly Father, it's all good, and it's all true. What else can you do but bow down and thank Him for His unlimited love? And then open your arms wide to receive it!

Heavenly Father, Your great kindness, compassion, and love are more than I deserve and beyond my wildest dreams. Help me humbly embrace all that You have given to me and all the blessings You have in store for me. Thank You, dear God, for numbering me among Your own. Amen.

What Everyone Knew

𝑵aomi's return with Ruth by her side was the talk of the town!
Wherever people gathered—in the fields, at the well, around
the courtyard of the synagogue, in homes—someone would say,
"Have you heard?" And once again listeners would shake their
heads to learn of Naomi's heavy losses and present poverty, and
puzzle over how Ruth's behavior disproved what everyone knew
about their heathen neighbors, the Moabites.

Yes, everyone knew Moabites were pleasure seekers, but Ruth
left many comforts behind to follow Naomi. Everyone knew about
Moabite women! They were shameless, brazen, and promiscuous,
but Ruth's demeanor exemplified modesty, grace, and humility.
Everyone knew that Moabites worshipped the false god Chemosh,
but Ruth worshipped the true God of Israel, the same God they
did. Ruth gave the people of Bethlehem much to talk about and
much to think about.

Boaz too had heard and learned. Whatever his opinion of
Moabites may have been, he recognized and honored Ruth for her
noble qualities. Her love and compassion for Naomi, a member

of his extended family, was more than word-deep. Her devotion to her mother-in-law proclaimed it more loudly than words ever could. Ruth's willingness to leave her old home behind and find a new home in the land of the God of Israel impressed him. How many, even among Israelites, would leave everything familiar to them if God should require such a sacrifice? Boaz remembered that the revered patriarch Abraham and his wife, Sarah, did exactly that. And now Ruth.

No Spirit-motivated, life-shaping decision we make for the sake of obedience to God's will is unimportant or insignificant. Small changes lead to major transformations! God sees when we're willing to leave what's familiar and comfortable—easy gossip, careless conversation, selfish choices—and follow His example of kindness, caring, humility, discretion, and selflessness. As our hearts change, so our everyday words and actions change. Others can't help but take notice because our lives are telling the story, loud and clear.

To follow God more closely, follow obedience to His will. Ask His Spirit to help you leave the old and enter the new in real, evident, and life-changing ways. The good things "everyone knows" about you will soon follow.

Lord Jesus, grant me the gift of obedience to Your will,
even when it means I need to change the way I think,
speak, or act. With Your Spirit at work in my heart,
let what people say about me prove a witness to
Your presence and power in my life. Amen.

A Godly Reputation

Choose a good reputation over great riches;
being held in high esteem is better than silver or gold.

PROVERBS 22:1 NLT

Ruth had no need to tell others what kind of woman she was. She owed no one an explanation of her beliefs and values or how she felt about Naomi, Naomi's people, and the God of Israel. Even though her identity as a Moabite cast her in an unflattering light among her neighbors, there was no need to defend herself with words. Her actions spoke for her.

Things haven't changed much, have they? Seeing is still believing when it comes to how we see others. We can hear eloquent protestations of love, but without loving actions, we have every reason to question the depth of that love. The same is true with any godly quality—kindness, compassion, honesty, integrity, faithfulness, trustworthiness. We can say all we want about ourselves, but people believe what they see us doing.

A good reputation among godly people isn't something we can talk our way into but naturally results when we act in obedience to God's will for our lives. Our love for others, our kindness toward everyone, is evident to all when we behave in loving ways on a daily basis; our character is unassailable when we treat others fairly, stand up for justice, and protect the weak among us not in words but in action. Faith in God is apparent when it's practiced.

It has been wisely noted that a good reputation is easier to maintain than repair. It's possible to lose a long-standing reputation for honesty with one shady deal; a well-earned reputation for kindness with a few mean-spirited remarks; an enviable reputation for decorum with one inappropriate outburst. Although we're assured of God's forgiveness and strengthened by His continuing love and guidance, we have repair work to do. We are compelled to apologize and make amends if possible, yet our day-to-day dealings with others from now on will say more than our words. Seeing is believing.

Look at your daily conduct from the point of view of others. What do they hear you say? What do they see you do? How do you think they feel after you have been with them—refreshed? Encouraged? Inspired? Uplifted? Loved? What do you have every reason to think your reputation is among them? Ask God where your obedience to His will may be lacking. Let His Spirit help you choose and maintain with visible action what is more valuable than any other possession—a God-pleasing and godly reputation.

Dear God, there are things I do, perhaps even unconsciously, that damage my reputation, and as a result, my credibility as a faithful and obedient woman of God. Open my eyes to see myself as others see me; grant me the power to change my behavior for the better. Amen.

Abundant Blessings

"The LORD repay your work, and a full reward
be given you by the LORD God of Israel, under
whose wings you have come for refuge."

RUTH 2:12 NKJV

*B*oaz blessed Ruth. Not only did he praise her for the devotion she had shown Naomi, but he also recognized that she had committed herself, an outsider, to the Lord God of Israel. Quoting from the sacred songs of Moses, he compared Ruth to a fragile eaglet and God to a mother eagle protectively spreading her wings over her nest to shield her young. Taught by Naomi, Ruth would have been familiar with the reference from holy writ.

Through faith, Ruth had put her present and her future into God's hands. While she was painfully aware of her weakness, helplessness, and dependence on the goodwill of others, Boaz reminded her of God's great love, power, and compassion. God watches over His own with the intensity of an eagle that quickly swoops down to catch the eaglet in danger of falling to the ground, he assured her. With wings spread out, He hovers over those who put their faith in Him. He covers them in the shelter of His arms. "In God," Boaz tells Ruth, "you have your strength. Be confident in the power of His might and the abundance of His mercy."

When someone we love is at a low point in life, there's no better encouragement we can offer than the blessing of God's eaglelike care, protection, and strength. To the believer, our words come as a refreshing reminder of His presence, even in the midst of struggles. Our voice may be the one God is using to soothe the fears of someone He cherishes. Our expressions of faith reinforce the faith of our sisters and brothers in Christ.

Those who do not know God's love for them need to hear words of this blessing too. It's possible that the hardships they are facing now are what God will use to arouse spiritual awareness or awaken their sleeping faith. It's only when we realize our weakness that we appreciate His strength; when we understand the depth of our need for Him that we allow His Spirit to lift our eyes up to Him.

Daily, God desires to bless you with the words of scripture. Let the sound of His voice remind you of His promises and fill you with confidence in His eaglelike care for you. Where could you use His strength? When would you appreciate knowing that His wings hover over you, shielding you from every spiritual danger? Let Him bless you richly!

Almighty God, thank You for Your many words of blessing to me. Use my voice to bring Your blessing to others, especially those who are feeling weak and helpless. Let my words uplift them, encourage them, and remind them of Your ever-present love and continuing care. Amen.

Why Pray?

Ruth replied, "Sir, it's good of you to speak kindly to me and
make me feel so welcome. I'm not even one of your servants."

RUTH 2:13 CEV

*B*oaz, as Ruth's protector, interceded on her behalf. He light-
ened her burden by providing for her safety while she gathered
grain in his field. He also spoke to God on her behalf, lifting her
faithfulness, devotion, and sacrifice to the throne of heaven. Didn't
God already know? Of course He did. But His Spirit at work in
the heart of Boaz moved him to speak of those who are admirable
and praiseworthy. While Ruth may have been hesitant to ask God's
blessing upon herself, Boaz took the lead. Where she might not
have known what to say, he did.

There are times when you might find yourself like Ruth—
longing for help but not sure how to pray. Somehow the words
don't come to you, or you're not sure what to pray for or pray
about. What is God's will for you in this situation? What words
would express how you feel right now? How can you bring the
needs of someone you love to the ears of your Heavenly Father?

Jesus is there to intercede for you. His Spirit, present in your
heart, speaks the words for you, even when you cannot. In your
sighs, Jesus sees your requests and brings them before your Father in
heaven. His Spirit blesses you with the certainty that your prayer has
been heard and will be answered according to God's will. You have
Jesus, the Perfect Intercessor, to speak on your behalf!

In faith in Jesus Christ, lift your voice to Him in prayer. Pray when there is a longing in your heart that you cannot name, a thirst in your soul that nothing can quench. Let Jesus plead for you. Pray for others. Be their intercessor, placing their spiritual and material needs at the foot of God's throne. Tell Him about the praiseworthy things they are doing.

Doesn't God already know? He knows better than anyone; but you don't know the depth of His care until you pray and watch Him work in your life and in the lives of others. You can't celebrate His work until you pray and see prayers answered in the most remarkable ways. You won't awaken to His presence until you pray and find Him beside you, speaking the perfect prayer, whispering His words of comfort in your heart. Pray so *you* can know!

In love, Jesus intercedes for you. In love, intercede for others. In love, rejoice in the privilege of prayer.

Thank You, dear Jesus, for speaking to my heavenly Father on my behalf. So many times I don't know what to pray for, and Your intercession assures me that my prayers always will be heard, even when I can't find the words to say, and answered according to Your will. Amen.

Come Here!

*At mealtime Boaz said to her, "Come here and eat some
bread and dip your morsel in the wine." So she sat beside the
reapers, and he passed to her roasted grain. And she ate until
she was satisfied, and she had some left over.*

RUTH 2:14 ESV

Time for lunch! A chance to sit in the shade, drink a cup of water, and eat a piece of bread must have come as welcome relief to the workers. People haven't changed much, so we probably aren't far wrong in picturing them fanning out in small groups of like-minded companions—bent, grizzled men; impish, energetic boys; wrinkled, work-weary widows; young, flirtatious women. Household servants apart from village gleaners; hired harvesters from poverty-stricken pickers.

But where did Ruth fit in? Custom and decorum would not put her among the men and boys, as much as they may have enjoyed her company. Her own reticence may have prevented her from joining a group of women, or perhaps she felt unwelcome among them. What Boaz may have seen was a lone woman quietly looking for a place to sit by herself.

"Ruth! Come here!" All conversation stopped as Ruth, eyes to the ground, quickly made her way to where the landowner and longtime members of his staff sat. Did she hear a murmur of displeasure as she passed by a group of gleaners? Would she have noticed the knowing looks exchanged by some of the harvesters? Feel the eyes of envious housemaids following her? Ignoring all this, Ruth answered the call. Boaz invited her to sit, eat, and enjoy his sumptuous fare. She was given all she could eat and more!

God is calling you to His banquet, where He will feed your soul with an abundance of spiritual delights. In His Word, the Bible, He invites you to know who He is and His gracious work on your behalf and in your life. He offers His standards to nourish your thinking, and His wisdom to sweeten your decisions and choices.

Among His people, your fellow believers, God provides you with many opportunities to worship Him, serve others, and mature in faith and understanding. At His table, Holy Communion, He bids you come—come here and share this meal with Me. Let your heart and soul overflow with His goodness!

Yes, there may be those who notice what you're doing and where you're going. Yet God calls them by name too. "Come here! Eat with Me!" And it might be your voice that He uses to call them.

Gracious Host, thank You for calling me by name to join You at your sumptuous feast. Stir my heart to come quickly! Grant me the privilege of being the one to call others to Your banquet so that their souls too may be fed to their full at Your table. Amen.

No Comment

When Ruth went back to work again, Boaz ordered his
young men, "Let her gather grain right among the sheaves
without stopping her. And pull out some heads of barley
from the bundles and drop them on purpose for her.
Let her pick them up, and don't give her a hard time!"

RUTH 2:15–16 NLT

*N*ow it's back to work. Ruth headed out with the others to the field. Of course, everyone noticed that Ruth was the object of Boaz's special favor. He made no secret of his attraction to the young widow, and he knew that his attention made Ruth the object of envy. After directing Ruth to the place where he wanted her to work, he ordered other workers to keep their comments to themselves.

In the workplace, in families, within congregations, and among friends, envy strains relationships. We notice when someone is singled out for special attention. Why them and not us? Envy spawns discontent with our own blessings, and breeds resentment toward the person we feel has surpassed us. Our feelings fester as we share in the gossip; we find ourselves among those who shun or undermine the one God has seen fit to honor.

During Jesus' earthly ministry, envy broke out even among His closest disciples more than once. Jesus firmly reprimanded them. They, like us, are reminded that God is the landowner and we are in His family and the workers in His field. What particular honors He bestows are entirely up to Him; whom He chooses to set aside for special work is His choice to make. From the rest of us? No critical, unconstructive comments allowed! Don't give these people a hard time!

Instead, support them. Celebrate the blessings God bestows on others, and encourage them and pray for them because they have received their blessings for a purpose. Support them by extending genuine friendship and speaking well of them among others. You will receive abundant blessings in return—to begin with, a heart free from the burden of desiring something that is not yours, plus a soul that marvels at the great things God does through all His people. Added will be contentment with what you have and gratitude for the work God has given to you. And the best of all is this: the worship and praise you give God in letting God be God.

God has honored you with a purpose in life. What He has given you to do fits into His plans, the good plans He has made for you. Be glad for His goodness to you!

Dear God, through the power of Your Spirit, enable me to turn thoughts of envy into words of encouragement and feelings of jealousy into actions of genuine friendship and love. Let me truly delight in the gifts of others and in the gifts You have given me. Amen.

Dirty Hands

Ruth gleaned in the field until evening.
When she threshed out what she had gathered,
she ended up with nearly a full sack of barley!

RUTH 2:17 MSG

*B*oaz was no absentee landowner. Yes, he certainly could have hired someone to endure the long days outdoors and spared himself the dust, sweat, and fatigue of fieldwork, but he didn't. He could have relaxed in the comfort of his house, but instead he walked among his workers, talking to them, overseeing the harvest, getting his hands dirty. At the same time, Ruth certainly would have preferred a good nap after enjoying Boaz's sumptuous meal! Rather than lingering in the shade, however, she returned to her humble, backbreaking work, feeling the sweat trickle down her face and getting her hands dirty gathering grain until evening.

God refreshes us when we spend time alone with Him in prayer, time hearing and learning His Word, and time reflecting on how His Spirit would have us apply His Word to our lives. But then we're called to do more than just think about it—we're called to get up and get going! In the field of our everyday circumstances, His Spirit reminds us to apply patience when standing in that slow-moving line; gentleness when confronted by a stressed-out coworker; compassion when responding to the child demanding our attention. We must get our hands dirty! We are His workers, and we have work to do in His fields.

God has not exempted Himself from the grit, challenges, and realities of this world. His Son Jesus was not content to sit in heaven and watch us suffer but walked among us so we would know that He truly understands our sorrows and cares about our struggles. Like Boaz, He was not afraid to get His hands dirty. In fact, His hands got more than a little dirty here on earth! His are the hands that were nailed to the cross for our sake.

Our risen Jesus lives today among us. Through His Spirit at work in our heart, He is out in the field with us, where there is still so much work to be done before evening comes. There's still the family member who feels alone, the stranger who hasn't seen a smile today, the friend wishing someone would call, the child who has no one to stand up for her, the neighbor who has never heard about Jesus.

After He has refreshed you, get up and go out into His field. Apply what you have learned from Him in the real-life situations you face every day. Don't be afraid to get your hands dirty!

Thank You, heavenly Father, for Jesus Christ, who was not afraid to allow His hands to be pierced for my sake. Never let me linger in the shade of pious imaginings, but show me how to apply Your Word to thoughts, words, and actions, and in my dealings with others. Amen.

Work for You

There are diversities of gifts, but the same Spirit.
There are differences of ministries, but the same Lord.
And there are diversities of activities, but it is
the same God who works all in all.

1 Corinthians 12:4–6 nkjv

There's no one just like you! So if you want to know what God's plan and purpose for your life is right now, you won't find it by looking at others and copying them. It won't come clear to you by taking on a task that you see as holy enough to please God. To discern God's will for you, all you have to do is look at you.

First, any desire or intention on your part that runs contrary to His teachings in scripture is not God's will for you. Yes, His love remains yours, and His invitation to seek His forgiveness is yours; but in going your own way, you forfeit the blessings inherent in obeying His commandments. When you intentionally fall short of His standards, your spiritual life languishes until you are ready to return to Him and accept redirection.

Second, God's plan for you will match the interests and abilities He has given to you. Someone else's talent may not be your talent, however much you may admire that person and his or her achievements. What are you interested in? What is the scope of your proven abilities? In what feasible way could you learn new skills, or strengthen and enhance the ones you already possess?

When your plan is God's will for you, He opens an opportunity for you to pursue it.

Third, ask yourself how you can use your current situation and your abilities right now to serve Him by serving others. God has put you (not someone else) where you are for a purpose. There's no time in your life that God cannot use you in some capacity, and everyone, including you, has a job to do. No one else is right where you are, meeting the specific people you will meet in the next several days and at the moment you will meet them. What you have to offer in the way of a warm smile, a friendly word, or a helping hand may be precisely what brightens their day. The gift of your time and abilities that you freely and generously give this week may help you better realize God's plan for your life—and uplift a few sorrowing hearts at the same time.

Today, give God your interests, gifts, and abilities, whatever they are. Pledge to Him your time and talents. Give Him you because He has a good plan for your life.

Thank You, Lord God, for the gift of my life and breath
and the unique interests, abilities, and opportunities
You have given to me. Open the eyes of my understanding
to discover Your good plans for me, and grant me the
desire to follow You with my whole heart. Amen.

Much More

*She took the grain to town and showed Naomi how
much she had picked up. Ruth also gave her
the food left over from her lunch.*

RUTH 2:18 CEV

What a windfall! Ruth went into the field that morning hoping to gather enough grain to make one or two loaves. She left with grain sufficient for twenty loaves. Not only that, she had a pocketful of roasted grain! Who would have thought such a bonus would come her way? It's as if we had hoped for a small, unadorned hamburger at best and were served a steak dinner with all the trimmings instead!

Ruth carried home more than she imagined she would ever get, yet she didn't hoard it in fear that such bounty would never come her way again. If it did, great; but if it didn't, that was all right too. Today she had received in abundance, and so today she would share in abundance. She brought everything home and spread it out in front of Naomi.

Imagine her mother-in-law's astonishment! Here she had sat all day long, wringing her hands with worry, blaming herself for not insisting that Ruth return to the safety of her family. She had heard stories of what could happen to vulnerable young women out in those fields. What if Ruth were teased, accosted, or. . .worse? If something happened to Ruth, could she ever forgive herself? Shouldn't she, an old woman, be the one out there gleaning? At least no one would bother her, she bitterly assured herself. Everything, everything was going against her.

Until now. Ruth did not come back frightened, wounded, or bruised. She wasn't in tears, regretting her decision to come to Bethlehem, and vowing to go back to Moab by any means possible. Stooped, sunburned, sweaty, and dusty she may have been; but her confidence was intact. Her satisfaction was evident. Her basket was full of grain. She was smiling! There had been abundance at noon for Ruth, and now there would be abundance in the evening for Ruth and Naomi together.

When the Lord blesses you with abundance, who else benefits? Who else is blessed for no other reason than the fact that you have been blessed? Certainly, the Lord serves you with the richest of spiritual food because He desires your strength, nourishment, and continued spiritual growth. But there's another reason He treats you so richly—it's so you can share with others. Those who are waiting for you to knock on the door of their hearts, enter in, and feed them with the love, compassion, and mercy of Christ.

Lord Jesus, thank You for the material and spiritual riches I possess because of Your generosity toward me. Now direct my heart to those who are waiting to be fed from my abundance. Through the power of Your Spirit, let me serve with the same generosity You serve me. Amen.

Blessings to All

Her mother-in-law asked her, "Where did you glean today? Where did you work? Blessed be the man who took notice of you!"

RUTH 2:19 NIV

Right away, Naomi realized that the grain Ruth brought back was no ordinary gleaner's haul. Someone had helped her bigtime! Yet without even knowing who, where, and why, Naomi gave God the credit, thanked Him with her whole heart, and asked His blessing on the person who showed such kindness to her daughter-in-law.

Not one of us could thrive emotionally, spiritually, or physically without the help of other people. As babies, we're completely dependent on our parents to take care of us, comfort us, and nourish us. Growing up, we rely on parents, guardians, pastors, and teachers to pass on to us their knowledge, experience, and wisdom. Our friends provide joy and relaxation, and later on, our neighbors, coworkers, and associates make it possible for us to contribute to and participate in our community.

God has placed people around you to benefit you, just as you benefit them. They make it possible for you to work productively and live with meaning and purpose, and you influence their success and happiness. Even those you have problems with further your growth in an important way! Without them, how would you know how patient, tolerant, kind, or compassionate God has made you?

The person who annoys or offends you is the same person who allows you to discover a weak point in your emotional growth. The one who makes unkind or critical remarks tests your spiritual maturity. But are they the ones you pray for?

In all likelihood, you readily thank God for those who make life easier for you. Who wouldn't? These are the people around you who notice you, encourage you, and provide their help whenever you ask for it. But at the same time, thank Him for the relative who's constantly complaining about something, the friend who just can't seem to arrive on time for anything, the clerk who bungles your order, the cashier who inadvertently overcharges you. How do you handle these things? What does your response to them tell you about yourself? If you would like to make a change for the better, thank God for them, and ask Him to bless them because it's through them that you are reaping spiritual riches. As the Holy Spirit motivates you to follow His example in all your interactions with people, things will change. You will grow in spirit, and they will see your example. Blessed are you!

With gratitude I come before You, heavenly Father, for all the people in my life each day. Thank You for those who notice me, who help, support, and encourage me; and thank You also for those who provide opportunities for me to reach out with Your understanding, compassion, and love. Amen.

House of Bread

Ruth told her mother-in-law about the one at whose place she had been working. "The name of the man I worked with today is Boaz," she said.

RUTH 2:19 NIV

*P*erhaps as the two women prepared their evening meal together, Ruth related in detail the events of the day. Here Naomi had spent the hours weighed down with worry, almost sick with desperation. But now, with every word that came out of Ruth's mouth, her anxiety lifted. Her hands relaxed into the familiar movements of making bread, savoring the welcome feel of flour between her fingers. For the first time since they left Moab, Naomi felt the warmth of human kindness. Indeed, Bethlehem—"the house of bread"—had provided abundant bread.

Only a short time ago, Naomi had been in the depths of despondency. The longer she let worry gnaw at her thoughts, the more hopeless her situation became in her mind. Would their nearest male relative do his duty and buy Elimelech's field *and* give her all the money from the sale? Perhaps she had reason to doubt his honesty. What about Ruth? What would become of the younger woman, the stranger in Israel, when the money ran out? While Naomi may have believed that she was being realistic, she actually was removing herself further and further from the facts. Yes, her situation was difficult, but fretfulness made it miserable. She didn't possess all power, but worry took away what little she had.

Worry is the opposite of faith. Throughout the Bible, God promises His presence, His care, His oversight, His protection. He assures us that He is in control. But worry makes us doubt His power over the events of our lives. Worry questions His wisdom in allowing us to go through such suffering and then suggests that our situation is without hope of ever improving. We agree because we've replaced faith in God's goodness with worry about His competence!

Think of a time you worried about the worst that could happen. Did it? Even if it had happened as you feared it would, you got through it, thanks to Almighty God's strong hand in your life. Chances are, however, that it didn't happen as you feared. Worry made you suffer needlessly. It gave you no power to change events or alter the outcome; it only took away the comfort God desires for you.

Through faith, God has led you to His house of bread. His Spirit will provide for the sustenance of your soul, and when your soul is fed, you have no hunger for worry. With Him there is hope—always hope.

Lord God, forgive me for the times I have succumbed to worry. Grant me the gift of faith that trusts Your wisdom and power. In my distress, help me look up instead of down, to You and not to my own imaginings. In You, I place my hope. Amen.

What's That Again?

"May the LORD bless him!" Naomi told her daughter-in-law. "He is showing his kindness to us as well as to your dead husband. That man is one of our closest relatives, one of our family redeemers."

RUTH 2:20 NLT

Hmm. . .Boaz, you say?" You can already tell that Naomi has regained control of her thoughts. While Boaz wasn't their nearest male relative, he was a close relative, and he was obviously favorably disposed toward Ruth. He was a man of power and influence, and perhaps he could convince their nearest relative to do right by her. Or perhaps that good man would buy Elimelech's property himself. Boaz would see that she received all the proceeds. A glimmer of hope emerged for Naomi as possibilities, even a long shot or two, rolled through her mind.

If Naomi had held on to God's continuing love for her and His promises, she would never have considered herself empty, as she did when she arrived in Bethlehem. Even if she could see no immediate way out of her unfortunate situation, trust would have given her the comfort of knowing that God remained in control. He had not forgotten her! She could have rested at ease in the knowledge that He would act in His time and in His way. And He did. Now that she had heard the name Boaz and learned of the attention he had shown Ruth, Naomi once again allowed God's comfort back into her life.

When we're fighting to make ends meet, battling a life-threatening health situation, or struggling against all odds, we want to give up hope. It's as if we're forced to navigate blindfolded through a dark alley, and the alley is full of twists and turns and dotted with potholes. But trust in God gives us this: His hand to hold on to and our Redeemer to lead us until He lifts the blindfold. There, right in front of us, is the end of the alley, bathed in light! And it's been there all along.

God shows you great kindness when He uses certain events in your life to teach you how to trust. By giving Him control, by leaning on Him as you step forward day by day, you learn how to walk in the dark. In His good time, you will see an opening, a ray of light. In His providential way, you will hear something that starts you thinking. *Hmmm. . .Boaz, you say?*

When you can no longer continue in the darkness, lean on Him, trust Him, because He will take you safely every step of the way.

Dear Jesus, sometimes hardship overwhelms me, and I just don't know what to do. Though I can't imagine any good coming out of what has happened, I know You can. Though I don't know where I'll end up, I know You do. Strengthen me with more trust in You! Amen.

Greener Grass?

Ruth told her, "Boaz even said I could stay in the field with his workers until they had finished gathering all his grain."

Ruth 2:21 CEV

Was the grass greener on the other side of the fence? Many harvesters and gleaners would have wanted to find out by migrating from field to field, always on the lookout for the easiest pickings and lightest tasks—and maybe the chance to work under a less strict foreman too. Those young men reprimanded by Boaz's overseer might have chosen to go where the men in charge wouldn't stand in the way of them having a little fun with the gals. Ruth, however, was advised to stay right where she was for the duration of the harvest.

At times we're tempted to go where we think the grass might be greener. We imagine our true happiness lies with a more attractive person, among other friends, or in some exciting new place. We might see "greener grass" over there where no one will say anything if we're acting contrary to God's rules; where we're not expected to meet God's standards; where we can choose what to believe and what not to believe, according to our personal judgment and point of view. That's where, we fancy, we will find our bliss.

What we don't see, however, are the dangers. When it's restlessness that takes us from one thing to another in search of what will make us happy, we're in for a sad awakening. After the thrill of something or someone new wears off, we're left with ourselves—still unhappy and looking over the fence again at what might lie elsewhere. Eventually we'll discover the truth of novelist Nathaniel Hawthorne's words when he said, "Make happiness the object of pursuit, and it leads us on a while-goose chase, and is never attained."

Spiritual restlessness too offers no better outcome, and it dims, even destroys, our relationship with God. Wherever His Word is reduced to pleasant thoughts and easy guidelines, it's true that we'll never hear a warning or a reprimand. But we will hear the voice of our own conscience, feel the unease of our spirit, and sense that we are not where God would have us. Yet how can we confess if everyone around us says we've done nothing wrong? How can we receive the comfort of God's forgiveness if we never admit to our failings? Where is God's peace here? The grass is not so green after all.

God graciously invites you to stay and work in His field. Give Him thanks because there's no greener grass anywhere than what you have right under your feet.

Dear God, thank You for inviting me to remain with You.
Though other choices may lure me, help me resist the
temptation to think I'll find good nourishment anyplace else
but with You. Let nothing draw me away from Your will,
because this is where my true happiness lies. Amen.

Wise Advice

"Good!" Naomi exclaimed. "Do as he said, my daughter. Stay with his young women right through the whole harvest. You might be harassed in other fields, but you'll be safe with him."

RUTH 2:22 NLT

Ruth didn't know what to do. Nothing in her life had prepared her to glean in the fields of Bethlehem! Perhaps a woman she had talked to that day mentioned gleaning in another field the next morning and suggested Ruth join her. The woman might have added that only Boaz's servants and hired workers stayed in his field through the entire harvest, but gleaners migrated. Yet Boaz himself had invited Ruth to remain in his field; and not only that, he had told her to work alongside the young women of his household.

Naomi seconded Boaz's advice. "Yes, no matter what anyone else does, you stay in his field," she said. "Work where he tells you, because that's where you'll be safe." Any questions Ruth may have had about what was expected of her vanished, and the matter of where she would go and what she would do the next morning was settled.

Wise advice is a blessing to receive. Whenever you're unsure what to do next, good counsel from a trusted, knowledgeable, and experienced friend or family member can help you make the right decision. Someone who knows you well, who can understand why you would feel the way you do, and who has your best interests at heart can allay your fears and respond to your misgivings. This person can answer your questions directly and honestly.

Wise advice is a blessing to give too. Your words can be the ones that counter timidity with confidence, doubt with certainty, hesitation with resolve, fear with courage, questions with answers. You could be the one whose good counsel keeps an immature or inexperienced person away from danger and encourages someone who needs a little help from someone who knows.

Wise advice blesses when it is not self-serving, offered with an ulterior motive, or given as an attempt to manipulate people or events. Wise advice never contradicts God's will and always promotes honest thinking and godly qualities, intelligent decisions and productive action. If what you hear, or find yourself saying, fails these tests, you know that what you're hearing isn't the best advice and what you're saying needs further consideration.

Be like Ruth—you will never hear wise advice unless you're humble enough to ask for it. Be like Naomi—others will never have the benefit of your wise advice unless you are caring and courageous enough to give it.

Lord God, thank You for those who care about me enough to tell me what they think is best for me. Thank You too for the privilege of giving advice when I'm asked. In my hearing and in my speaking, enable me to respond and act wisely and well. Amen.

Marvelous Plan

She kept close to the young women of Boaz, gleaning
until the end of the barley and wheat harvests.
And she lived with her mother-in-law.

Ruth 2:23 esv

Ruth and Naomi were assured of provisions through early summer, when the wheat harvest would end. This gave Naomi time to focus on the future. Though the Law of Moses provided for widows through their kinsman-redeemer, their nearest male relative, not all men lived up to their responsibilities. Besides, Ruth, as a foreigner, had no legal protection whatsoever. Her only hope lay with Naomi's being able to receive the proceeds from the sale of Elimelech's land, which would be a finite amount and not likely to last through the younger woman's lifetime. While Naomi pondered these facts, Ruth walked to Boaz's field every morning and returned with grain every evening.

God was accomplishing His marvelous plan for Ruth and Naomi, but it's unlikely either woman even caught a glimpse of it as they dealt with their day-to-day needs. It's no different for us today! When we settle into an ordinary routine—getting the kids ready for school, commuting to work, going to class, attending meetings, fixing meals—we think nothing special is happening. Sure, we know that God is present, but in the absence of any dramatic turn of events, we imagine He's just letting us coast along from day to day, year to year, with no particular plan in place for us at all.

You might suppose He's all out of marvelous plans, as He's used them up on people like Ruth and Naomi! But God's plans are beyond your imagining. By not expecting Him to do anything special, you miss the daily signs of His active presence, His continuing care, and a glimpse of His ongoing plan and purpose for you.

Spiritual seasons turn and change, each with its own beauty, its own reason. God grants you springtimes of discernable growth, robust refreshment, and increased realization of His truths. There are summers of exuberant joy, friendship, laughter, and love. You feel capable and confident, encouraged and optimistic. And there are also autumns of unsettling change, nagging doubts, shadowed thoughts, and difficult adjustments. You may experience winters of sadness and sorrow. But if you have ever seen a cold, frigid landscape, you know that new growth is quietly forming underneath the snow. You know that the miracle of another springtime is not far away.

No matter what season, open your eyes to God's hand in it. Watch as He accomplishes His marvelous plan for you, day by day, every day.

Dear God, help me perceive Your marvelous work in my life. When I think nothing's happening, grant me eyes to see the miracle of every day. When I imagine You have nothing left for me, lift my heart and soul to the reality of Your continuing presence, Your awesome love. Amen.

Wait on Him

One day her mother-in-law Naomi said to Ruth, "My dear daughter, isn't it about time I arranged a good home for you so you can have a happy life? And isn't Boaz our close relative, the one with whose young women you've been working? Maybe it's time to make our move."

RUTH 3:1–2 MSG

*N*aomi had hatched a plan. Her former pessimism had lifted, and she began see to an opportunity that was almost unimaginable before. She wasn't blind to the fact that Boaz was physically attracted to Ruth, treating her with far more attention than even compassion demanded. Was marriage a possibility? It was a long shot. While Boaz obviously admired the pretty young woman, he might not consent to marry her. He was an Israelite, and she was a foreigner. Yet if a marriage were to take place, Ruth's future was assured. If a son would be born to Ruth, he would inherit Elimelech's property, bringing it back into the family and providing for Naomi's support and well-being.

Something as small, as fragile, as an older man's attraction to a younger woman was enough to make Naomi think these things. But was it God's will? At the end of the harvest season, perhaps Boaz, a man of many responsibilities, would forget all about Ruth. Shouldn't Naomi go directly to her nearest relative and demand her rights and forget this wild dream? No, she decided; be patient, be patient. Their nearest relative had shown no interest in the widows' plight. Meanwhile, Boaz had. He was worth the wait, and she would wait until just the right time.

Most of us have trouble with patience—we don't like to wait. Accustomed to instant answers and quick turnarounds, we're taken aback when what we want doesn't happen immediately. We'll do anything rather than endure days, weeks, months of uncertainty, often accepting a decisive no today rather than holding out for a possible yes later on.

Yet patience pays off when we let God work, act, and move in His own time. Through the cautionary words of others, He may tell us to wait until we receive more information, more understanding, more resources before going ahead. His Spirit may speak through a sense of hesitation or uncertainty on our part, prompting us to move a little more slowly because the right time hasn't come just yet.

Take your ideas and desires, hopes and plans to Him. With Him, all things are possible. But if you don't perceive an opening or it's not the right time yet, wait. Wait patiently on Him.

Heavenly Father, waiting is hard for me, especially when there's the possibility of a great blessing coming into my life. Enable me, through the power of Your Spirit, to trust Your timing. Grant me the grace to accept Your yes or no, because You always have my best interests at heart. Amen.

Everything to Gain

Let us come boldly to the throne of our gracious God.
There we will receive his mercy, and we will
find grace to help us when we need it most.

HEBREWS 4:16 NLT

Nothing ventured, nothing gained"—the saying was true for Naomi, and it's just as true for us today. Naomi's forthright venturing was no foolhardy gamble, however, but a calculated risk that she was willing to take based on the facts she had gathered and the customs of the time. She knew that Boaz was a devout man who worshipped God in word and action. She knew that he observed and upheld God's laws, as well as the time-honored traditions of Israel, his family, and his community. So when Naomi presented her daring idea to Ruth, she had every reason to believe that, whatever Boaz decided, Ruth would come to no harm.

Yet for all his many virtues, Boaz was still a human being, subject to weaknesses and temptations, mistakes and stumbles, the same as everyone, then and now. Naomi's plan, though based on observable realities and the long-established duties of a kinsman-redeemer, still carried with it an element of risk.

Risk of any kind is absent, however, when you venture out to Jesus, your divine, ever-present Kinsman-Redeemer. Kinsman? Yes. When the Holy Spirit brought you to faith, you entered God's family. Jesus calls you His sister. Redeemer? Yes. His death on the cross and resurrection from the grave fulfilled God's justice on your behalf.

Jesus has redeemed you—bought you back—from the poverty of not knowing your Heavenly Father or having a relationship with Him. Through His work of redemption, Jesus made it possible for you and all believers in Him to receive His grace, mercy, and compassion, no matter how sorrowful the heart, how bleak the situation.

Do you find yourself hesitant to approach your Lord? Perhaps there are memories of past offenses that hold you back; current conditions that keep you from seeking His presence; or feelings of unworthiness that tempt you to turn away at the last minute. Yet Jesus has willingly taken on the role of your Kinsman-Redeemer, and He has obligated Himself to carry through with all the duties and responsibilities that come with the title. As true man, He understands your needs, longings, weaknesses, and desires. As true God, He possesses the power to come to your aid without fail. You have nothing to risk in venturing into His presence right now, and you have everything to gain today and forever.

Thank You, dear Jesus, for willingly taking on the role of my Kinsman-Redeemer. Enable me, undeserving though I am, to boldly and confidently place myself in Your presence as I read and reflect on Your Word, grab hold of Your promises, and receive Your complete forgiveness and overwhelming grace. Amen.

Dress for Success

"Tonight he will be winnowing barley on the threshing floor.
Wash, put on perfume, and get dressed in your best clothes.
Then go down to the threshing floor, but don't let him know
you are there until he has finished eating and drinking."

RUTH 3:2–3 NIV

Matchmaker Naomi had it figured out. If all went according
to her plan, Boaz would remain in the field after the harvest
ended to guard the grain. Of course, many landowners wouldn't,
but Naomi knew that Boaz was a conscientious, hands-on manager. It's possible too that she had heard talk among the women
drawing water from the well that Boaz intended to stay out in the
field that night.

Naomi instructed Ruth not to join in the evening's meal or
end-of-harvest festivities but to wait until most everyone else had
gone away and night had fallen. That's when Ruth, cleaned up
from the day's work and dressed in her best, would approach Boaz.

To our thinking, Naomi's plan sounds like outright seduction.
Let's look more closely, however. Given Ruth's relationship by marriage to Naomi, and by extension a family relationship to Boaz, she
was claiming a right due her as a family member (although not as
a foreigner) under the laws and customs of the time.

Up to this point, Boaz the boss had known Ruth as a field-
worker, although one he particularly favored. He had seen her

dressed only in rough, drab work clothes; he had watched her work, stooped over, gathering fallen grain. But now it was time for him to see Ruth in a larger role. She would present herself as Ruth, a widow and member of his extended family, who was petitioning him to become her kinsman-redeemer, protector, and guardian. Ruth, following Naomi's instructions, would perform an action tantamount to a proposal of marriage.

As a member of God's family, you too have a new, larger, and more meaningful role than simple existence. You are no longer living for yourself alone but as a witness to the joy and peace you have received through the gift of His Spirit. While those who know you may have seen you one way in the past, your words and actions today compel them to look at you with new eyes. Though you may never have imagined that your daily activities have significance beyond yourself, God says they do.

Today, let His Spirit clothe you in robes of patience, humility, compassion, selflessness, obedience, and love for others. Let the sweet perfume of your heartfelt prayers touch the heavens. Let Him dress you for true and lasting success!

Dear God, open my eyes to see myself in the role
You have for me, and help me understand all that You
would have me do as Your beloved child. Let all my
thoughts, words, and actions conform to Your will
because I belong not to myself but to You. Amen.

Squeaky Clean

*If we live in the light, as God does, we share
in life with each other. And the blood of his
Son Jesus washes all our sins away.*

1 JOHN 1:7 CEV

*a*ll the dust and grime of the day disappeared as Ruth carefully washed herself. A large earthenware bowl filled with water, perhaps heated over an outdoor oven, as well as a sponge, would have done the job; or she may have walked to a nearby stream and bathed there. Either way, she would not appear before Boaz stained with the dirt of the field because she wanted to him to see her as a new woman, a woman worthy to stand in the presence of a highly respected man.

Similarly, as the Holy Spirit awakens us to the darkness of our natural condition, we draw back from the radiant presence of God. We realize that the soil of sin permeates our thoughts, words, and actions. Is this a difficult truth? Yes, but by denying the obvious fact that there's evil in this world and sinfulness in every heart, we only delay the cleansing God has made available to us. Like petulant children, we'd rather live caked in mud rather than take a bath!

The mystery of Jesus' atoning sacrifice on the cross, the blood He shed, is the living water that we can come to every day. It washes away the guilt of sin from our soul and grants us the privilege of standing before our Heavenly Father robed in purity, perfection, and holiness. The cleansing power of His complete forgiveness removes all traces of shame from us, and we can appear before Him with confidence because He sees us without spot, as He is.

Many of us try to make ourselves God-clean by resolving to not let mean thoughts enter our mind or careless words cross our lips. We commit ourselves to patience, kindness, gentleness, and obedience to all God's commandments. But natural inclinations continue to blemish even the most saintly among us. We can never get ourselves clean in His sight, and that's why, from the first sin in the Garden of Eden, God said, "Let me do it. Bathe yourselves in the living water I will send, and you will be clean."

As you wash your face in the morning, remember the washing that Jesus provides for you. When you shower each day, recall the soul-deep cleansing available to the heart aware of its true condition. Reflect on the sacred significance of baptism and the earthly water used to symbolize heavenly renewal and restoration. Let Him bathe you in the living water of His love.

Lord Jesus, bring me to the cleansing waters of true repentance for my sins, and bathe me in the assurance of Your complete forgiveness. Thank You for removing the stain of my sins so that I can stand before You, confident that I am truly acceptable in Your sight. Amen.

Good Reputation

*Watch where he goes to spend the night, then when
he is asleep, lift the cover and lie down at his feet.
He will tell you what to do.*

RUTH 3:4 CEV

*N*aomi held Boaz to high standards. She trusted that when he found Ruth lying beside him, he would not take advantage of the situation. She relied on him to remember that God sees, and even the deepest darkness of the night cannot hide sin from His eyes. She depended on him to correctly interpret Ruth's actions as a proposal of marriage, which was acceptable at the time, given Ruth's need and his position.

In that Boaz wasn't Naomi's closest male relative, however, it was a proposal he could decline. If he had done so, Ruth could have appealed to the closer relative, and if she were an Israelite, that man would have been obliged to marry her and father an heir to Naomi's land. But since Ruth wasn't an Israelite, he could have refused her plea with no repercussions.

This night, the godly reputation Boaz had earned and maintained would be sorely tested. Would what he did in private prove as honorable as what he did in public? Would he adhere to the same moral principles that he demanded of others? One overheard whisper was all it would have taken to start the smirks, the knowing looks, the wildfire rumor that could shatter Boaz's reputation, as well as Ruth's, as soon as the first rays of the morning sun fell across the harvested fields.

An upstanding, God-honoring reputation takes time to build. Only daily dedication to the well-being of those around us will earn us a reputation for being a responsible person, just as only constant hard work can bring about a reputation for diligence. Others hear not just our words but our tone of voice and attitude. They see what we do, and they form opinions about our character, reliability, and loyalty. Our private behavior has a way of making itself known, and our reputation rests on what others know about us.

Yet all it takes is one notable stumble to ruin a good reputation of long standing. People hear or see something that calls into question everything they thought they knew about us. Will they forgive us? With a straightforward confession and genuine apology, we're likely to receive forgiveness from others, and we're certain to receive it from God. But now it's our task to regain their trust and re-earn their respect, and that takes a long time.

Are you serious about guarding your good reputation? Is there anything you do that potentially could damage it?

Father in heaven, where others praise me, enable me to live up to their good opinion of me. When I falter, grant me a spirit of sincere repentance and the humility to beg their forgiveness. Help me each day to deserve a reputation for honesty, integrity, kindness, and truthfulness. Amen.

Compassionate Plans

"I know the plans I have for you," declares the
LORD, "plans to prosper you and not to harm you,
plans to give you hope and a future."

JEREMIAH 29:11 NIV

Naomi's plan reached far beyond her own well-being. A fair price for Elimelech's field would have provided enough money for her to live on for the rest of her days. But she had more than herself in mind. First, there was Ruth. Because she was a foreigner, no one was obliged to marry her or provide for her. Second, there was the land, closely tied to the preservation of Elimelech's family name. Right now, it was under someone else's ownership. If Naomi died without producing an heir (and at her age that was a likely prospect), and should a kinsman-redeemer refuse to do his duty, the field would be attached to another family member's holdings.

Now if Boaz were to marry Ruth, at the very least, Ruth's upkeep, as well as Naomi's own, would be assured. It was almost unfathomable that a man of Boaz's stature would treat either of them badly. At most, Ruth, still of childbearing age, would have a son who could bring the property back into Elimelech's family, thus continuing Elimelech's name through his descendants. If that happened, the met needs of the day would carry blessings far into the future—as indeed they did in the story of Ruth.

Compassionate plans take others into account. Although we may have something in mind that would accomplish a goal or fulfill a dream of our own, our carrying it out might affect other people, often in significant ways. A self-serving decision on our part could disrupt the lives of those dependent on us, especially the weakest and most vulnerable among us. A voluntary, self-motivated change in our lives could take us away from our God-given responsibilities or remove us from where God, in His wisdom, has placed us. To one extent or another, there are few significant choices we can make that do not touch the lives of others in some way, good or not so good, for the better or for the worse.

Your best plans, your compassionate plans, include yourself and also go beyond yourself. These plans consider the obvious needs and reasonable feelings of those around you and weigh the probable consequences of your proposed actions. You may find you can carry them out in good conscience or that there is room for adjustment, compromise, or postponement to protect the weak and vulnerable. Pray, then, that all your plans—like Naomi's plans—pass the test on all counts!

Lord God, I lay before You things I'd like to do. Grant me wisdom to make compassionate decisions when what I want to do would diminish the lives of others, especially those who are helpless. May my plans reflect the good plans You have for me and those I love. Amen.

A New Land

She said to her, "All that you say to me I will do."
So she went down to the threshing floor and did
according to all that her mother-in-law instructed her.

RUTH 3:5–6 NKJV

Ruth could not be expected to understand the intricacies of Mosaic Law. Though Naomi surely explained Israelite customs and traditions, they must have come across as strange and puzzling. We might excuse the foreigner if she had cried, "I don't get it!" and walked away. We'd understand if she had told Naomi, "I'm listening, but it doesn't make sense to me, so I won't go along with it." In reality, Ruth, realizing her lack of knowledge, obeyed her wise mother-in-law and did everything Naomi had told her to do.

Today, some of God's warnings and guidelines sound puzzling to us. More accustomed to letting current values lead our thoughts and actions, we're taken aback when God, through His Word, our conscience, or a caring Christian friend, steps in and tells us, "No, do it this way." Sometimes we completely reject the advice. Although we claim to live according to God's Word, we do so only as long as what He says makes sense to us.

But spiritually, we are foreigners living in a strange new land. In His Word, God reveals how we are to conduct ourselves in this place, what we're to do in certain situations, and which choices and decisions reflect His principles and values. Of course, we are here on earth, and He is explaining to us the holiness of heaven! Will we always understand why we're to live up to His high standards? No, but our wise God knows. In obedience to Him, we'll do everything He asks to the best of our ability.

Often, as we gain experience in the world, we discover for ourselves why God made a specific rule, and we're glad and thankful that we followed it, even though at the time we didn't understand. As we'll see as Ruth's story progresses, that's exactly what happened to her. God's blessed purpose for her life unfolded as she obediently followed Naomi's instructions. In later years, how she must have looked back and smiled to remember how odd it all sounded to the inexperienced young woman from Moab!

Each time you hear God's Word, or listen to the stirrings of His Spirit in your heart, or pay attention to God-given advice from mature Christians, you're learning the ways of your new land— God's land of spiritual joy and peace. Enabled by His Spirit, you obey because you believe He knows what He's talking about.

---

*Lord God, let Your commandments guide my ways as
I learn how to live a God-pleasing life. Help me accept
what is true, right, and holy, even when I don't understand;
grant me the desire to persevere and let Your perfect will
unfold through the events of my days. Amen.*

Brave Steps

*After Boaz finished eating and drinking and was feeling happy,
he went over and fell asleep near the pile of grain. Ruth slipped
over quietly. She lifted the cover and lay down near his feet.*

RUTH 3:7 CEV

Naomi had told Ruth to remain unobserved until all the men staying in the field were ready to call it a night. She watched as they finished their meal and separated, each finding a spot near stacks and bundles of harvested crops. Following Naomi's instructions, Ruth noted where Boaz went to lie down. Only then did Ruth make the move that would either make her a disreputable, fallen woman or a married, protected woman. She would know soon enough.

This wasn't the first time Ruth had taken a brave step into the unknown. Over ten years ago, she had married into a transplanted Israelite family. Would her Moabite family and friends desert her? Would she be accepted by her Israelite mother-in-law? Would she find their moral standards—much more demanding than those of Moab—difficult and intimidating? Far safer to marry the Moabite man her mother and father had in mind for her! Yet Ruth let her love for Mahlon lead her, and she stepped into marriage not knowing the outcome, good or bad.

And then Ruth was faced with Mahlon's death and Naomi's decision to return to Bethlehem. Far safer to remain in Moab, where her prospects for remarriage were bright. She was still young, attractive, and desirable. Even Naomi pointed that out. But Ruth loved Naomi, and she wanted to worship Naomi's God, so she insisted on going to Bethlehem. Would she be welcomed or shunned? Would she soon become one of them or remain the outsider forever? And among all the eligible Israelite women, why would an Israelite man pick her to marry? Highly unlikely! But again, Ruth let love lead the way, and she took the brave step of leaving the familiarity of Moab behind and going with Naomi into the strange land of Bethlehem. What would happen to her there, she left in God's hands.

When has God called you to take a brave step into the unknown? Perhaps it was the time you steeled yourself to attend church again after a long absence; the time you spoke to a friend about your faith in Jesus Christ; the time you let love lead you to obedience to His Word. Each time you took that step, He strengthened you to take another. Who knows what God-given, thrilling, and fulfilling brave step is waiting for you? Don't be afraid to take it!

Grant me courage, dear God, when I step into the unknown. Let me put my hand in Yours when the way seems dark and strange, and fill me with confidence when Your direction for my life takes me where I wouldn't normally go. Keep me next to You! Amen.

How Far?

At midnight the man was startled and turned over, and
behold, a woman lay at his feet! He said, "Who are you?"
And she answered, "I am Ruth, your servant. Spread your
wings over your servant, for you are a redeemer."

RUTH 3:8–9 ESV

I am your servant." Ruth's humility is evident, even as she carries out her bold and courageous act. No matter what happens, she won't forget the kindness that Boaz has shown to her. He had shielded her from harassment as she worked in his field, and he had made sure that she took home more than enough grain for herself and Naomi. Would he be willing to do even more? "I plead for your continued protection," she tells Boaz. "You, as a man with the power to buy back those in your household enslaved by misfortune, can marry me. You can free me forever."

Was she asking too much of this good man? To what extent was he willing to fulfill the role as kinsman-redeemer in Bethlehem? Hadn't he done enough already? Was there a limit to his kindness, his generosity, his obligation to Naomi's widowed daughter-in-law? It was up to Boaz to decide.

Many of us who desire to follow God's Spirit put a limit on how far we will go. At the onset, we're delighted to practice acts of kindness to others and give generously to those less fortunate than ourselves. It's exciting, and it feels good! The first time we hear someone praise our patience, helpfulness, or dedication, we're pleased, inwardly thanking the Holy Spirit for bringing us to this point of spiritual growth.

But then comes the day that God asks us for more. He wants us to repent of a particular sin, overcome a long-standing weakness, or give up one of our favorite guilty pleasures. It could be He nudges us to share more of our income with the poor at home and missions abroad or invites us to spend more time in Bible reading, study, prayer, and reflection. Perhaps He calls us to speak out more clearly and forcefully about our faith or stand up for someone who has been unfairly criticized, cruelly treated, or unjustly accused. God leaves it up to us to decide just how far we're willing to extend ourselves for the sake of our life in Him.

With God, it's never about what you can or can't do but what you're willing to do. When He asks, He knows you have the power to do it because He gave it to you. How far will you go with Him? He leaves it up to you to decide.

Dear God, when Your Spirit invites me to do more,
give more, be more, grant me the courage and willingness
to say yes. Help me rely on You to give me everything
I need to ably carry out Your desires and faithfully
follow wherever You might lead me. Amen.

Under His Wings

Keep me as the apple of Your eye;
hide me under the shadow of Your wings.

PSALM 17:8 NKJV

S pread your wings over me!" Ruth's words echoed the words that Boaz had spoken to her. Upon learning of her devotion to Naomi and desire to worship the God of Israel, Boaz had prayed that the Lord God, "under whose wings you have come for refuge," would bless her abundantly (Ruth 2:12). Her request also alluded to a common Hebrew idiom, "spread the wings of your garment over me," referring to the bond of marriage.

For us, God's promises are the wings He spreads over us. He has made us His own through our Spirit-planted faith in the life, death, and resurrection of Jesus Christ. In Him, we're shielded from fear because He has pledged His confidence to draw on and His arm to lean on. Under the cover of His protective Word, we're nourished by His Spirit, renewed by His forgiveness, and emboldened by His invitation to come to Him in prayer. He promises to strengthen us in times of weakness, comfort us in times of sorrow, and bless us with His spiritual gifts. Love, joy, kindness, self-control—all these He creates in us, enabling us to live joyfully according to His will.

Imagine you are Ruth, the helpless one, pleading with the only person who has the power to meet your needs. What would you say? Would you talk about health, finances, or troubled relationships, either your own or those of someone you love? Would you bring up the distressing thoughts that you can't seem to chase out of your mind, worries that are all too real to dismiss, fears you have never admitted to anyone else?

Would you beg for the faith, hope, perseverance, and commitment you need to reenergize your life? Courage to follow Him more closely? Assurance of His forgiveness? Comfort of knowing you have a place in heaven? Would you dare to share your critical material needs and your deepest spiritual needs with someone who is willing and able to supply all these things and more? Yes, of course.

The story of Ruth and Boaz reflects your relationship with your Heavenly Father. Like Ruth, you have real-life needs, both material and spiritual. Like Boaz, God has put Himself under obligation to come to your aid; He has the power to provide for you, and He is willing to do so. He desires to come into relationship with you, protect you, and spread the wings of His promises over you. Will you ask Him to do that for you? Be like Ruth, and insist on it.

---

*Heavenly Father, thank You for making it possible for
me to approach You through Jesus Christ with all my
needs, the needs of those I love, and the needs of the world.
The more I pray, the more I come to know You as my
Provider, Protector, and Redeemer. Amen.*

The Right Way

*"The LORD bless you, my daughter," he replied. "This kindness
is greater than that which you showed earlier: You have not
run after the younger men, whether rich or poor."*

RUTH 3:10 NIV

*B*oaz got the message! Again he blessed Ruth, this time with
even more emotion because her actions displayed extraordinary faith in the God of Israel. Here she was, a foreigner who not
only embraced Israelite laws and customs but was also willing to
put them to the test. She risked her honor, safety, and reputation,
trusting that God would guide Boaz's response. And Boaz indeed
responded to her according to His will. Instead of seeing a promiscuous Moabite woman, he saw a true daughter of God.

Ruth's coming to Boaz in boldness and confidence came as
a great compliment to him. Though her behavior stemmed from
her trust in God, it also reflected her trust in Boaz as an honorable
man who would adhere to God's commandments under all circumstances. Her actions demonstrated her complete reliance on
him for her protection and well-being and showed that she recognized his power to provide for her needs. Her words called upon
him to exercise his authority as kinsman-redeemer and make her
his wife. Ruth did everything God's way, and it was the right way.

Boaz acknowledged the compliment. With it, she repaid
the respect he had shown her with complete respect for him. While
young women of lesser maturity would have selected someone

younger, more handsome, and less serious than Boaz for a husband, Ruth preferred the God-fearing man worthy of her love. She knew where genuine, enduring commitment could be found and returned.

So often, we attempt to meet our needs on our own. We may have a particular goal in mind, a particular dream we want to make real, but do we first take it to God in prayer? Do we pay Him the compliment of asking Him to grant it, believing He has the power to do so, and then relying on His response? Not always. It's all too easy to simply go for it, using our own means and reasoning, even brushing aside a few of God's guidelines in the process, if that's what it takes. But even if we get there, we're not where God wants us to be spiritually. And if we don't, perhaps that's what it takes for us to do it the right way—God's way—next time.

How do you go about seeing to your needs, finding meaning and purpose in your life, discovering fulfillment, and achieving your dreams? Follow God's way and you'll be going about it the right way.

---

*Almighty God, as I lay before You my hopes
and dreams, enable me to truly trust in You to do
what You know best. Let me rely on Your wisdom to
shape my actions and Your power to bring about
the blessings You have in store for me. Amen.*

In God's Family

"Now, my daughter, do not fear. I will do for
you all that you ask, for all my fellow townsmen
know that you are a worthy woman."

RUTH 3:11 ESV

It mattered who Boaz married. He was born into the messianic line of Judah, meaning that among his descendants would come God's promised Messiah. Who knows? Maybe his son would be the long-awaited one! It would have been the prayer of any devout Hebrew man, particularly a man in Boaz's position. The ideal wife for Boaz would have been a pious Hebrew daughter from a God-fearing family that, like the family of Boaz, could trace its ancestry back to Judah, the son of Jacob, son of Isaac, son of Abraham; and Leah, the elder of his two wives. Boaz was an older man; it's possible that there had been such a marriage, with Boaz left a widower and without children.

Ruth opened Boaz's eyes to a truth God has revealed repeatedly throughout sacred history and continues to reveal to us today: He calls His children by name, by the faith in their heart, and not according to where they were born, the way they dress, where they live and work, what they're able to do, or how they appear to us. Ruth's faith and the actions prompted by her faith told Boaz all he needed to know: in his presence was a true daughter of Abraham who was eligible to join him in marriage.

Perhaps you find it hard to believe that, by faith, you are

Abraham's offspring also. Maybe there's someone you know who cannot see himself or herself as a beloved member of God's family. There are struggles with feelings of unworthiness; assumptions of disgrace because of past sins; or assumed disqualification due to personal limitations, background, or present circumstances. But see what Boaz saw in Ruth! If he had looked with human eyes, her lineage would have been a deal breaker. Sweet woman but no marriage, no way. Yet because he was willing to look beyond the surface, he saw her faith, and he found that faith, and faith alone brings people into the family of God.

Your Spirit-planted faith has made you a member of God's family. Do others see you that way? If they fail to accept you as a true daughter of God, perhaps it's your words and actions, commitment and dedication that God will use to open their eyes to the truth. By faith, you are a daughter of Abraham. By faith, you belong to Him.

Lord Jesus, thank You for making me a member of Your family. Though I am helpless to bring myself to You, You chose to see me in the light of Jesus Christ and call me Your own. Now let my thoughts, words, and actions reflect my faith in You! Amen.

Firm Foundation

*"While it's true that I am one of your family
redeemers, there is another man who is more
closely related to you than I am."*

RUTH 3:12 NLT

oaz needed to dot all the i's and cross all the t's. There was a man
more closely related to Elimelech who had first dibs on the land,
according to the law. In addition, while the letter of the law didn't
give him the duty to marry Ruth and father a son in Elimelech and
Mahlon's name (it applied to the brother of the deceased husband),
the spirit of the law would have included this moral responsibility.
After all, the law's purpose was to provide for widows and keep
land in families. If Boaz were to prematurely announce his intention to marry Ruth, it could be interpreted as a land grab on his
part. He planned to prepare a firm foundation, legally and morally,
for their future.

We put our plans on a firm foundation when we proceed the
way Boaz did—thoughtfully and deliberately. The short time it
would take Boaz to consult Naomi's next of kin could save days, if
not years, of disputes. It would stave off ill will, gossip, and resentment that could permanently tarnish the couple's reputation. Consideration for the rights of others, and regard for both the letter
and spirit of the law, help us lay a good foundation for what we
want to accomplish.

Jesus' parable about the wise man who built his house on rock and the foolish man who built on sand illustrates the importance of setting our faith on a good foundation. It's insurance for our future! Faith without a strong, solid foundation stands more on personal feelings than on God-given fact, so when feelings change, we begin to doubt the reality of God's presence, forgiveness, and love. Confidence in God's power gives way if our circumstances change, say, from good fortune to hardship, from everything going our way to significant life challenges.

Faith built on the truths of God's Word, however, withstands life's chances and changes. It's marked not by drifting feelings, lofty thoughts, and spiritual ideals but by firm belief coupled with practical action. Firm-foundation faith can't help but express itself in the way we treat other people, react to adversity, and respond to the world around us. Firm-foundation faith is built on the words and teachings, commandments and guidelines given by God in scripture.

The Holy Spirit has given you a foundation of faith in your heart. Are you allowing Him to strengthen it by reading His Word and embracing His promises? Is it evident in your peace of mind and in visible, practical action?

Heavenly Father, open me to the building work of Your
Spirit in my heart. Replace hazy hopes with solid fact,
changeable feelings with firm faith in everything You have
revealed in scripture. Let this faith express itself in all
I think, say, and do, and in how I treat others. Amen.

Stay Here!

"Stay here for the night."

RUTH 3:13 NIV

Dawn was hours away. Boaz and Ruth sat together in one of the far corners of the field where a dark and dangerous path lay between them and town. It was no place for a woman alone; besides, Bethlehem's gate would have been closed at dusk, so she would need to rouse a guard to enter. You can imagine the talk among the townspeople as soon as Ruth's midnight appearance became known! The only good choice was for Ruth to remain where she was until she could return home discreetly and safely.

Spiritually, there are dark and dangerous paths that wisdom begs us not to take. "Stay here!" God's Spirit says when we're tempted to act outside God's clearly expressed commandments "just this once." We hear His Spirit's warning when we indulge in self-centered fantasies instead of God-centered thinking; when we substitute the world's standards for God's standards; when we venture into the night to find happiness rather than staying in the sunlight of His joy. His Spirit cries, "Stay here!" when we're drawn into the captivity of man-made rules to earn God's favor instead of relying on the freedom Christ's death and resurrection has won for us.

As you grow in His grace, there will be times when His Spirit says, "Stay here! Rest awhile with Me. Let Me nourish your heart and soul before you venture out into what I have prepared for you." You may be eager to get things started, just as Ruth and Boaz no doubt were. Yet for them, nothing could take place until the morning, when Ruth could return home and Boaz could see to the legal matters at hand. "Stay here!" is His Spirit's word to you when things just aren't ready yet for your next step.

Also, you will often sense the stirrings of His Spirit nudging you to take a step into a dark-to-you path. Say He moves you to take on a project that will ease the burden of someone else, or spend more of your time helping others, or find out more about Jesus and His ministry. This is a dark, unknown path as far as you're concerned! But with Him at your side, you can walk in complete safety and confidence.

What do you hear Him saying to you today? If it's, "Go ahead," then get going! But if it's, "Stay here," wait patiently. Trust Him to know the right time for you take the next step in fulfilling His will and purpose for you.

---

*Dear God, thank You for the gift of Your Spirit to
direct my way. Enable me to hear His voice, and grant
me the willingness to follow His direction. In Your love,
give me both the patience to wait here and the confidence
to go forward, according to Your will. Amen.*

Good as Your Word

"In the morning, if he wants to exercise his customary rights and responsibilities as the closest covenant redeemer, he'll have his chance; but if he isn't interested, as GOD lives, I'll do it. Now go back to sleep until morning."

RUTH 3:13 MSG

In God's sacred name, Boaz pledged to help Ruth. He didn't know what complications, if any, his pledge to her would entail. Nevertheless, he was going to perform in the light of day what he promised in the darkness of night. No matter how things turned out, Ruth and Naomi would be taken care of and the land purchased.

Words of promise from others to us, and from us to others, allow us to share deep feelings and serious intentions. "I'll take care of that project" from a coworker relieves you to focus on other tasks. "I'll be there for you" from a friend means that you are not alone in bearing a burden or facing a challenge. "You can depend on me" from a loved one allows you to rest easy today and not worry about tomorrow.

Of course, a promise is only words if it dissipates with the passage of time or disappears at the first hint of inconvenience. Sometimes others let us down, and sometimes we let others down. In our interactions with others, we learn very quickly whose promises we should treat with skepticism and whose promises we can take to heart. Sure, when a promise is made, we may not know; but time reveals the truth.

Boaz was as good as his word, and God's Spirit leads you to the same level of integrity in your daily life. Say you promise a child that you will take her to the playground this weekend; an employer that you will not reveal company strategies; or a beloved friend that you will marry him. They can depend on you because they know that you're as good as your word. You will keep your promise to the best of your ability, barring circumstances that make it impossible or unwise for you to do so. That's Boaz-style integrity!

In the privacy of your heart, what promises have you made to yourself? Perhaps you have promised that you will adopt a healthier diet, exercise more often, go back to school, or set a worthwhile goal on the job or in your community. Maybe you've promised yourself that you will work harder from now on—or take more time for rest and relaxation with family and friends. Consider the promises you've spoken in your heart. Are you as good as your word to yourself?

Dear God, You promised to send Your Son to bring heaven's love to earth in visible form, and You did. Help me follow through on the things I promise to myself and others, even if it proves inconvenient or takes extra time and effort on my part. Amen.

Time for Everything

*She lay at his feet until morning, and she arose before one
could recognize another. Then he said, "Do not let it be
known that the woman came to the threshing floor."*

RUTH 3:14 NKJV

She longed to shout it from the rooftops! How glorious it would
feel to tell the other young women about Boaz's awesome
promise to her! But Boaz cautioned Ruth not to speak to anyone
she might meet as she slipped away just as dawn was breaking.
"Go home as unobserved as possible," he cautioned. "Tell Naomi,
of course—share with her the promise I have made to you, but tell
no one else for the time being. Our reputations and the success of
my plans rest on your discretion." Boaz's words anticipated those
of Solomon when the wise king observed that there is a time for
everything under heaven, including a time to keep silence and a
time to speak.

Untimely talk often circulates suspicions and suppositions as
truth before they're proven false or misleading. Then what? Retrac-
tions, corrections, and explanations follow but hardly make a dent
in what "everyone knows." Social media has made it all too easy
and all too tempting for us to speak at times when silence is the
better course.

Our words matter because words can influence or even change
the way people view someone we've spoken about or an event
we've discussed. For the brief moment we enjoy being first with

the story, we pay dearly in embarrassment for having gotten it wrong. In our personal relationships, we may discover that others hesitate to share a confidence for fear that we will not respect their privacy and dignity. In business, we may find ourselves excluded from important meetings because we're not viewed as someone who can be trusted with sensitive information.

As there is a time to keep silence, there is also a time to speak. Just as we often speak about our interests and the doings of our family members, we are invited to speak about how God has made us members of His family. To our friends and relatives who have yet to know God as their loving Father, we can tell about His creative power and His great compassion for all people. To those who find themselves burdened with guilt and grief, we can share the forgiveness and peace that Jesus Christ has waiting for them. To anyone looking for moral guidance, personal direction, and the meaning and purpose of life, what better conversation could we have but one about the Holy Spirit's work in every believing heart?

There is a time for everything.

Lord God, through listening to You, I receive
guidance and wisdom. Let me apply it to my life so
I may discern when to remain silent and when to
speak up. In all things, dear Lord, let my words help,
not hinder, Your work in the world. Amen.

Here and Now

*He said, "Bring the garment you are wearing
and hold it out." So she held it, and he
measured out six measures of barley and put
it on her. Then she went into the city.*

RUTH 3:15 ESV

*G*reat things lay in the future! But there was still the here and now, and Boaz hadn't forgotten. No matter what would take place later and whatever the outcome of his pledge, Ruth and Naomi still needed food today. So he supplied it abundantly. Ruth went home with a full shopping cart, thanks to her generous benefactor.

Long-term strategies to alleviate hunger and other great social ills promise relief tomorrow, yet there are people in need today. And though we may believe we'll be in a much better position to offer help in the future—when we get a higher paying job, have more free time, acquire influence in the community—our good intentions lift no one's burden right now. Sure, our capabilities and opportunities may well increase in years to come, but why wait? A little practical help that we can give now can ease a present need.

A monetary donation to a charity, a sack of canned goods for the food pantry, or an hour or so of volunteer work? Excellent! But there are other daily needs that can become so familiar, so routine, that we may not even see them as needs. We tell a child who wants to show us a drawing that we'll look at it later, as we're pressed for time right now. Tomorrow we plan to see if we can run an errand for a homebound friend, yet she needs groceries today. We'd certainly like to visit our parents more often, check in on the elderly neighbor who seems so lonely, if only we weren't in such a hurry. Maybe later, okay?

Your thoughts about the future—where you would like to be, what you would like to find yourself doing—provide direction for your life. Without short- and long-term goals in mind, you wouldn't be able to make choices and decisions today that support these goals. Unless you dream, you won't know what you can do to make tomorrow's intentions a reality. But if you fail to notice daily needs within your power to supply, or dismiss them as less important than your plans for the future, you might send Ruth away hungry. "Our main business is not to see what lies dimly at a distance," the nineteenth-century author Thomas Carlyle wrote, "but to do what lies clearly at hand."

What lies clearly at your hand today?

Thank You, dear God, for meeting my needs every day.
You are never late with the whisper that turns me away
from danger, the word that gives me encouragement,
the help that I couldn't do without. You generously
provide everything I need at just the right time! Amen.

His Way

The LORD God has told us what is right and what
he demands: "See that justice is done, let mercy be
your first concern, and humbly obey your God."

MICAH 6:8 CEV

The story of Ruth is all about people. Even though they lived at a time and in a place far from our own, their experiences have relevance for us today. Though they had individual identities and different roles, Naomi, Ruth, and Boaz had one thing in common—each, in his or her own way, wanted to follow God. Isn't that the desire of every believing heart?

In how she acted toward her Moabite daughters-in-law, Naomi followed God by treating Ruth and Orpah with kindness, the way she would want to be treated. For Naomi, God's rules for family relationships weren't ideals kept in a cabinet and brought out only for special occasions but put to use in real-life circumstances every day.

Boaz knew all the laws handed down from Moses governing the obligations of landowners to workers; wealthy householders to destitute beggars; and heads of families to needy relatives. But he spent no time looking for loopholes that would excuse him from his responsibilities. Case in point—he could have claimed no kinsman-redeemer responsibility toward Naomi, as there was a closer male relative. He also had no obligation to Ruth, a foreigner. But Boaz followed God by paying attention not just to the letter of the law but the spirit of the law also.

Ruth was not raised to know God's commandments, but as she came to faith in Him and learned of His love for her, she asked, "How can I follow You, Lord?" In response, His Spirit opened her eyes to the opportunities around her. So she loved and respected her husband and her mother-in-law. She allowed her compassion for Naomi to take her to Bethlehem. She adopted a humble, thankful attitude, and she continued to work hard even after Boaz had shown her special attention. She accepted wise advice, doing exactly what Naomi and then Boaz told her.

If you want to know how to do the things God wants you to do, you need look no further than the opportunities around you right now. What does His Spirit point out to you? Perhaps a self-image that could more reflect God's love for you; an attitude that could be sweetened with genuine gratitude for your blessings and gifts; words that could be chosen with a little more care and consideration; feelings toward others that could more resemble God's love for you. How to follow God? The answer lies within you.

Dear God, help me embrace all the ways I can follow You. Grant me willingness to do what You should ask of me, however humble the task. I know that You do not look at the earthly status of the act but the humility of the heart that performs it. Amen.

Thriving Relationships

When Ruth went back to her mother-in-law,
Naomi asked, "What happened, my daughter?"
Ruth told Naomi everything Boaz had done for her.

RUTH 3:16 NLT

Ruth could keep a confidence, but she was not secretive. Once she and Naomi were in private, Ruth told her mother-in-law precisely what had taken place that night. You can imagine the excitement in Ruth's voice, along with a hint of awe that her mother-in-law had conceived such a strange-sounding but successful plan. In her heart, Ruth must have felt extraordinarily thankful she had followed Naomi's instructions exactly, despite her natural reservations and misgivings.

And think how Naomi felt! Picture her listening in rapt attention to everything Ruth said. The weight of anxiety she had suffered under all night lifted; relief poured over her, flooding her heart with gratitude for her daughter-in-law's compliance, Boaz's integrity, and God's answer to her fervent prayers. Naomi had been right about Ruth, about Boaz, and about God.

Healthy, wholesome relationships thrive on openness. Friends and loved ones we trust with our inmost thoughts are the ones who have shown over time that they love us deeply. We place our hopes and dreams in their hands, and they treat them seriously and thoughtfully. While we share our successes with many people, we reveal our failures only with those who are closest to us because we know for sure they'll love us anyway.

We learn where to place our trust only by trusting. Of course, sometimes we're going to get it wrong and find ourselves sorely disappointed, perhaps even nursing a broken heart. Is forgiveness possible? It's not only possible but essential to the healing of our hearts and for the health and well-being of other relationships, current and future. If we don't forgive and don't allow ourselves to trust others, we'll never truly open up to anyone. The more we keep to ourselves, the less we share with others; and the less they know of us, the less apt they are to grow close to us. We're left with many acquaintances but no heart-deep relationships.

Your Heavenly Father invites you to be open—completely open—with Him. Sure, He's God and He knows everything about you, even things you don't know about yourself! But suppose your best friend went through a life-changing event but chose not to tell you about it. Now she knows and you know; but her silence in front of you prevents you from sharing your understanding, thoughts, and compassion. Be open with God! Trust Him with every detail, and let your relationship with Him thrive.

Heavenly Father, please send Your Spirit into my heart so that I may learn to trust You completely and without reservation. Through the gift of Your beloved Son to bring me into relationship with You, You have shown Your never-ending care for me and all I am and do. Amen.

More than Enough

*She also said, "Boaz gave me this grain, because he
didn't want me to come back without something for you."*

Ruth 3:17 cev

*B*oaz stood in second place as kinsman-redeemer to Naomi,
but he occupied first place in taking care of her. He sent Ruth
home with grain enough for two, specifically mentioning Naomi.

Many of us might find it gratifying to put ourselves in Boaz's
place. He was able to give generously from his bounty to two needy
people so humble, so thankful, so worthy of his help. But how
about standing in Ruth's place? We're less comfortable envision-
ing ourselves among those who are completely reliant on another
person to provide for them. After childhood, we're accustomed
to getting out there and working for what we need, earning our
own money, and controlling our own destiny. If someone gives us
a gift, we feel obligated to reciprocate with a gift of equal value. If
someone does us a kindness, the first thing we want to do is find a
way we can return the favor.

Social norms and expectations, however, can cloud our true
position before our God. Before Him, we are needier than Ruth!
We depend on Him for everything, not only our daily bread but
our daily breath. We rely on Him alone for the strength and power
to live as spiritual people, as strangers trying to make our way in an
unbelieving world. We lean on Him for wisdom, understanding,
and discernment. Without His Spirit working within us, our souls

would starve for lack of nourishment.

How comfortable are you being Ruth, the needy receiver? How do you accommodate the fact that everything you possess now is from God and everything you will possess in the future will come from His hand? It's impossible to give Him anything He hasn't given you in the first place. You can't return a gift of equal value because the whole world, the whole universe, belongs to Him. He created it! So how do you feel asking God for all your needs? More importantly, how do you feel receiving His blessings, the abundant, overflowing, more-than-enough blessings He showers on you?

In front of Boaz, Ruth made no show of self-sufficiency but humbly asked for what she needed. When it was given to her, she responded with gratitude, recognizing the source of her blessings and honoring the generous giver. Ruth is an example for every faithful heart. God invites you to come to Him with your needs and desires, hopes and dreams. Ruth shows you how to receive what He gives you.

Thank You, Lord God, giver of all good things.
Create in me a heart overflowing with gratitude for
Your care for me and with joy for all the love You have
shown me. Let my response to the needs of others reflect
the way You meet my every need. Amen.

Wonderful Prayer

I sought the LORD, and He heard me,
and delivered me from all my fears.

PSALM 34:4 NKJV

I sn't it wonderful when God gives us exactly what we pray for? He did that for Naomi!

When Ruth left Moab and came to Bethlehem in Judea, she entered as an alien with no right other than to gather grain at harvesttime in the fields of landowners. Naomi took responsibility for her daughter-in-law's well-being, and making provisions for Ruth's future was essential. For a woman, that meant marriage. And what better marriage could Ruth make than with a near-relative of Naomi's, a man who had shown her such kindness? So that's what Naomi prayed for. And then she prepared a plan to see if perhaps this was God's will. Yes, it was His will; events were unfolding more smoothly than she could have imagined.

What made Naomi's prayer so effective? First, Naomi's prayer was generous. She wasn't focused solely on her own needs but on another's needs. Second, Naomi's prayer was active. Not asking for a miraculous fix to fall from heaven, Naomi put to use the knowledge and position she had, working within the laws and customs of the time. She prepared a practical plan that, if it worked out, would assure Ruth's future as well as her own.

Third, Naomi's prayer was humble. She knew she didn't control God! She certainly had not prayed for the famine that drove her husband, sons, and herself away from their family and friends. She never prayed for her sons to marry non-Israelite women. She didn't pray for her husband and sons to die in Moab but that the family would return to Bethlehem someday, healthy and prosperous. There her sons would have married, and she, in her old age, would be a grandmother many times over. But God had other plans then, and Naomi knew He might have other plans now. She would embrace whatever answer she received.

If you want to hear God's yes when you pray, pray for those things He has promised in His Word—faith and forgiveness, His mercy, comfort, and compassion. He promises wisdom to all who ask, so pray for the wisdom to see His ways and discern His path for you; pray that your prayers reflect His will, and then rejoice as you watch Him at work in your life. Most of all, pray with a humble heart. For Naomi, God had a plan more wonderful than she could have imagined. For you, He has a wonderful and full-of-wonder plan too. It unfolds with His every answer to your prayers.

Dear God, let my prayers be pleasing to You. Grant me a generous heart, as eager to pray for others' needs as I am my own; make me willing and eager to do what I can, quick to get to work; and give me a humble attitude, accepting Your will in all things. Amen.

Worth the Wait

Naomi said, "Sit back and relax, my dear daughter,
until we find out how things turn out; that man isn't
going to fool around. Mark my words, he's going
to get everything wrapped up today."

RUTH 3:18 MSG

*N*aomi and Ruth had done all they could do. Naomi had devised a practical and realistic plan to get what she most desired— marriage for Ruth and Elimelech's field back in the family. Ruth had followed Naomi's advice, and she returned home with a full report. Had the women attempted to do more, they would have been stepping far outside the boundaries of their authority and social custom. The matter lay in Boaz's hands, as he was the only one in a position to carry things further. "Wait!" Naomi told Ruth, and she spoke wisely.

Most of us have been in a position similar to that of Naomi and Ruth. We did all we could do, and the outcome rested with someone else who possessed the ability, authority, power, or resources to take things further. It was hard to wait! But waiting taught us important truths about our lives together. It highlighted our mutual dependence on others and reminded us to use our position and influence to help those who cannot help themselves.

Waiting teaches us important spiritual truths too. For example, we learn that God promises us love, joy, peace, patience, kindness, goodness, faithfulness, gentleness, and self-control. He gives each of us gifts of the Spirit, enabling us to fulfill the plans and purposes He has for us. Yet tired at the end of the day, we're less than kind to the person who cuts in front of us on the highway. Annoyed at being interrupted, we snap at the person who called. Not chosen to lead the Bible study, we feel slighted. So He *doesn't* give us the promised gifts?

He gives them, but there's a "Wait!" that comes with them. Love, joy, peace—all these gifts are yours, but they build with time, experience, and spiritual maturity. Does it feel like two steps forward, one step back? Sure, but all the while you're learning to use God's spiritual gifts in real-life situations and apply them in your responses to the people around you. Your stumbles open you to receive His forgiveness as He lifts you up and dusts you off. You're ready to begin again, this time with the gifts of increased wisdom and strength.

In all things, do what you can, and then wait. Give others the privilege of helping you. Give God the opportunity to be God. You'll find it worth the waiting!

Almighty God, You aren't looking for an overnight saint but a day-to-day disciple willing to grow as You nurture, learn as You teach, and understand as You reveal Yourself. Let me do everything within my power and then wait on Your timing. I leave every outcome to You. Amen.

PART 3:

Ruth and Boaz at the Threshing Floor

What's Happening?

Boaz had gone up to the gate and sat down there.
And behold, the redeemer, of whom Boaz had spoken,
came by. So Boaz said, "Turn aside, friend; sit down
here." And he turned aside and sat down.

RUTH 4:1 ESV

"So what's happening?" With the advent of cell phones, our question gets an instant reply. Ubiquitous portable video cameras and other recording devices have made it possible to watch events unfold on the other side of the globe in real time. But Naomi and Ruth had no way to communicate with Boaz as he tended to the business at hand, nor he with them. Even though their future was being decided, Naomi and Ruth could not know what had taken place until Boaz or his messenger came and told them.

If they could have looked, the women would have seen Boaz walking to the gate of Bethlehem, a walled town. As in other towns and cities of that time and place, men gathered at the gate to chew over the goings-on of the past day, seal business deals, and in all likelihood, talk about the weather. You could be sure that someone you wanted to see would pass by on his way to his fields outside the city walls. While Naomi and Ruth were trying their best to go about their household duties, Boaz was positioning himself where he knew Naomi's next of kin would appear. The man came by, and Boaz invited him to sit down. He had a business matter to discuss.

Like Naomi and Ruth, you remain at home, unable to accompany God as He puts in place the events and circumstances that affect your life. "What are You doing, God?" is a cry that may come from your heart when you wonder what, if anything, is happening. Naturally you fret when you don't see movement where you expect movement. God remains unresponsive to your questions concerning the means He is using to bring you to where He wants you to be, physically, emotionally, and spiritually.

In many instances, God's actions are closed to you. No text message arrives to keep you up to date on the ways He is working in the minds of those who are making decisions that touch your life and in the hearts of those coming into your life to bless, help, and encourage you. It's possible that, unbeknownst to you, His Spirit is using your waiting-on-God time to draw you closer to Him in trust and confidence, to strengthen your faith, and to deepen your joy! What is He doing for you? Everything!

Dear God, thank You for the ways You work for my good. Let me trust You with my whole heart because I know You are true to Your Word. What You say will happen, happens. Let me wait in patience for the time when You reveal Your work to me. Amen.

Real Compassion

Boaz called ten leaders from the town and asked them to sit as witnesses. And Boaz said to the family redeemer, "You know Naomi, who came back from Moab. She is selling the land that belonged to our relative Elimelech."

RUTH 4:2–3 NLT

How could this man *not* have known Naomi who came back from Moab! Bethlehem was a sleepy rural community where everyone knew everyone else. Naomi's arrival after ten years' absence and Ruth's sudden appearance was major news, and the widows' sad plight was no secret. Legally, the man Boaz addressed was the closest kinsman and therefore responsible for Naomi. He should have opened his door to her and her daughter-in-law. Yet he had made no move to even inquire about her needs. Boaz, although not obliged to do so, had stepped forward with compassion and kindness, providing practical and timely help.

Why did this man turn a blind eye to Naomi's suffering? Probably for some of the same reasons we are often blind to the burdens of those around us today. Like the neglectful kinsman, we get caught up in our own doings to the point that we don't even notice the needs of others who are right around us. The homeless man on the corner we pass every day becomes part of the landscape!

Then again, suppose we're aware of someone's unfortunate situation and have the power, even the responsibility, to help change things for the better. But we don't get involved because help often means spending our time or giving our money. Do we really want to do that? Now, at this moment? While we're willing to offer them words of heartfelt sympathy, and we might even name them in our prayers, we hold back when it comes to following up with timely and practical help that we have the ability to provide. It's very possible, however, that ours are the hands God wants to use to reach out to that person today.

God may never ask you to rescue a whole village from dire poverty, but He may stir you to spend time with a grieving friend, mentor a struggling middle-school student, make a regular donation to a charity, or volunteer at a food pantry, community garden, or animal shelter. If you see a need, why not?

What you do to turn your feelings of compassion into actions of compassion shows you've noticed. What you do to back up sympathetic words with practical help shows you understand. What you do to relieve someone's suffering shows you care.

Heavenly Father, Your compassion for me led You to send Your Son into the world to make Your presence real to me. You express Your kindness in the material and spiritual blessings You pour on me daily. Enable me to make my care for others real in their lives. Amen.

Working Together

*"I thought I should bring the matter to your attention
and suggest that you buy it in the presence of these seated
here and in the presence of the elders of my people."*

RUTH 4:4 NIV

Together the men would settle the matter of Naomi's field. Boaz went in front of the town elders because they were the ones appointed to decide on and legalize property sales. In addition, should a dispute arise at a later time, Boaz and his challenger could call on these respected witnesses to judge the validity of their claims. Boaz had a legal and a practical reason for not trying to do everything on his own but to get others involved.

As God leads you toward deeper and fuller spiritual understanding, the presence of others enriches your journey, just as you enrich theirs. Say you see how much value a friend finds in attending Bible class or a home group study, and you decide to join. Of course, reflecting on God's Word in the privacy of your heart is important and necessary; yet when you add your insights to the insights of others, together everyone's knowledge and understanding increases. Or suppose a coworker notices your consistent patience, calmness, and kindness when you respond to difficult people and manage tense situations in the workplace. She asks you how you remain so poised and peaceful, and then you tell her about the presence of God in your life. Together, you have a meaningful conversation about how God's Spirit nourishes His gifts in the hearts of those who love Him.

Working with others brings you the satisfaction of contributing your perspective, your experience, and your abilities to accomplish worthy goals. Could anyone in the group do it all by herself or himself? No. Even if one person is responsible for most of the effort or provides the bulk of the resources, the presence of others serves as needed support and assistance, inspiration and encouragement. Together, you can reach more, achieve more, and do more.

God has put you among others. He never meant for you to single-handedly fix all the world's problems but to get together with like-minded people and contribute your time and talents. He doesn't expect you to fulfill your purpose in life by yourself either; instead, He puts others around you so you can share your hopes and joys, fears and misgivings, celebrations and successes. Even the productive criticisms and thoughtful comments of others help you get better and go further as a faithful disciple of God.

In what ways could you work more smoothly and joyfully with others?

Lord God, help me see where I can work better by working with and among others. Show me how I can more generously give of my time and talents and more joyfully and thankfully receive their encouragement, inspiration, and offers to help. Grant us all the privilege of working together! Amen.

No Problem!

*"If you will redeem it, do so. But if you will not, tell me,
so I will know. For no one has the right to do it except you,
and I am next in line." "I will redeem it," he said.*

RUTH 4:4 NIV

Sure, I'll buy the land—no problem!" Juggling numbers in his
head as he spoke, the would-be buyer figured he could nab this
one on the cheap. How much money does a woman need, anyway?
He exchanged knowing glances with a few of his cohorts gathered
around. Naomi was too old to bear another son to claim the property, so if he threw a few coins to the widow, the field would be
his, free and clear.

It's easy to step forward when we have little to lose. Who
wouldn't jump at the chance to bask in the admiration of others
while doing nothing meriting praise? To earn maximum wages for
hardly lifting a finger? To enjoy a reputation as a kind, honest,
and compassionate person without performing kind, honest, and
compassionate actions? To possess soul-deep joy, divine wisdom,
and spiritual peace by spending mere moments in the presence of
God, the source of joy, wisdom, and peace? No problem, we'd say.
"Count me in!"

Experience, however, reveals the truth. In everyday life, we
know that genuine respect is won with respectable behavior;
rewards come with the time, attention, and effort we give to our
work; kindness, honesty, compassion, and forgiveness are real in

our lives only insofar as we apply these heavenly qualities in down-to-earth encounters.

God's presence? Of course, we're always in God's presence because God is everywhere! But awareness, appreciation, and wisdom come when we get to know Him as He makes Himself known to us. He fills us with His joy, and He covers us with His peace. But how can we receive His joy if we're still looking for instant happiness in worldly experiences and material things? How can we receive His peace if we keep running to denial, addictions, forgetfulness, and false promises?

Ask someone you know who has followed God's way for many years. Hear the truth before you commit yourself. Listen when this person tells you that God's Spirit may stir you to speak kindly even when a clever, well-deserved retort burns on your tongue. You may find it necessary to forgive the person who is unapologetic, unremorseful, even belligerent. For the sake of following through with following Him, you might find yourself going against popular notions, perhaps even the firm opinions of close family and friends. Pray for the faith that makes it "No problem!" for you!

When I have promised to You far beyond my capacity to deliver, Heavenly Father, forgive me. Grant me, I pray, the strength I need to increase my commitment to You. Make my heart teachable so my faith will become real in practical ways and in real-life situations. Amen.

Growing Delightfully

Unlike the culture around you, always dragging you
down to its level of immaturity, God brings the best
out of you, develops well-formed maturity in you.

Romans 12:2 msg

Long ago, we wanted to watch TV, play a video game, go out with friends. But parents insisted we finish our homework first. We had hoped to breeze through all our high school classes, but a certain teacher demanded more. She challenged us, and we struggled to earn a decent grade in the class. In traffic court, we thought we could talk our way out of a speeding ticket, but the judge held us accountable, and we faced the consequences.

At the time, these encounters were far from delightful. Yet they shaped our character and instilled positive qualities. We realize now how much more satisfying life becomes when we possess the discipline to put first things first; the self-confidence of knowing we can succeed if we try; and the ability to consider the probable outcome of our choices and actions. All those hard lessons of the past, and the ones we are still learning today, make us better able to navigate our way through life. Paradoxically, it's not by taking the easy way, drifting along with our whims, that our highest hopes become reality. It's by reaching for a goal beyond ourselves and doing what it takes to get there.

As we grow in God's Spirit, we go through times that aren't delightful. Work is required! And this is when some of us fall away, choosing to do something else rather than spend more time in God's Word. We get discouraged when God's truths aren't immediately open to us and call for further reflection. We give in to bitterness or cynicism when we've had to learn a lesson the hard way—by experience. Yet these are the very things that build us into confident, mature, and effective Christians. They're vital to our spiritual development because without them we remain in spiritual infancy.

Today, recall some of the valuable lessons you learned while you were growing up. Think about a time you took on a challenge and overcame it or struggled to reach a worthy goal and made it. Thank God for those times! Thank Him also for the hurdle you're facing right now. How do you think God is using your situation to shape your character, build your confidence, strengthen your faith in Him, and enrich your spiritual understanding? Take delight in this evidence of His Spirit at work in you!

Thank You, Heavenly Father, for caring for me and loving so much that You continue to lead me onward to increased spiritual wisdom, maturity, and understanding. Teach me Your ways, dear God, and make me willing to keep learning and keep growing, no matter how old I am! Amen.

Ideal Stand

Boaz said, "The day you buy the field from the
hand of Naomi, you also acquire Ruth the Moabite,
the widow of the dead, in order to perpetuate the
name of the dead in his inheritance."

RUTH 4:5 ESV

*N*ow comes the kicker. The deal isn't as simple as it first appeared. The original Hebrew in which the book of Ruth was written uses a phrase that could mean that the buyer of the field was obligated to marry Ruth and sire an heir for Elimelech's field. If this is the case, Boaz was insisting that the next of kin observe the spirit of the law, just as Boaz himself was prepared to do. (By Mosaic Law, this duty fell to brothers only.) Should Ruth bear a son to inherit Naomi's field, any future sons born to her would be entitled to inherit part of the buyer's estate—an estate he was guarding for his own children. It's possible too that the man was repulsed at the idea of taking a Moabite into his family.

The phrase also could be interpreted to mean that once the man purchased Naomi's field, Boaz would marry Ruth. Now a son born to them would have an overriding claim to Naomi's property! Naomi would have no obligation to return the money her kinsman had paid for it. If Ruth bore a son the next year, the most he would get is one harvest out of it before ownership shifted to Ruth's son, with Boaz as caretaker until the son came of age. In barely a year's time, the buyer could find himself with no field and no refund.

Either way the phrase is taken, the information Boaz delivers causes the kinsman to think twice before sealing the deal. The high standards that Boaz set effectively thwarted the would-be buyer's gleeful plan to take advantage of Naomi's misfortune.

Often, it takes only one person's honorable behavior to shame someone with unethical, self-serving plans in mind. Your stand for what's right is indisputable proof that everyone doesn't lie, cheat, or steal. Even if there's nothing you can do to stop someone from taking a moral shortcut, the fact that you don't makes an impression. Later on, as the other person reflects on what happened, they might have regrets. It's possible that this person had not lived up to their ideals, and your courageous stand reminded them.

Opportunities to live your ideals rarely announce themselves with a trumpet blast. Instead, they appear nestled wherever there's a "kicker" in everyday conversations, common transactions, even private decisions. What does your response tell others about you?

Dear God, forgive me for the times I have not lived up to my ideals. I have let selfish interests dictate my behavior, and I am sorry. Send Your Spirit into my heart so I may begin again this day, refreshed by Your forgiveness and strengthened by Your goodness. Amen.

Do It Yourself!

*The man answered, "If that's the case, I don't want to buy it!
That would make problems with the property I already
own. You may buy it yourself, because I cannot."*

RUTH 4:6 CEV

Do it yourself!" That's the answer Boaz was hoping for, and the one he expected. It cleared the way for him to take on all the responsibilities of Naomi and Ruth's kinsman-redeemer.

The story of Ruth helps us better understand Jesus' work as our Lord and Savior. Though most of us are not completely powerless in society, as Naomi and Ruth were, each of us was born with a sin-prone nature. As we grew from infancy, we became more and more aware of the attraction of "me"—the appeal of getting our own way, the allure of selfish desires. We learned that there's a difference between right and wrong; even if no one were to teach us, our consciences would tell us. We also found out that despite our best intentions to do otherwise, we give in to temptation, and when we do, we feel guilty.

Many of us try to get rid of guilt by ourselves. Perhaps we make excuses, saying we really didn't mean to do what we did; adjust our consciences, claiming what we did wasn't so wrong at all; or justify ourselves, deciding that God, like a doting grandfather, overlooks our shortcomings.

But there's no lasting peace here or in any other way around personal guilt that we can come up with. Like Naomi's suddenly unwilling kinsman-redeemer, self-made peace fails to follow through and fails to liberate us from the discomfort of guilt. There comes a time when we're forced to admit we can't rely on anything else to free us, and that's when we search for someone who can and will—our divine Kinsman-Redeemer, Jesus.

Jesus, as true God and true man, is the only One with the power and authority to atone for our guilt. Long ago, on a hill of blood outside the walls of Jerusalem, His death on the cross tells us in no uncertain terms that sin is serious in God's eyes. Jesus' resurrection from the dead three days later shows us in glorious fact that He has atoned for our sin and forgiveness is ours. Peace is ours, and He took on the job Himself, gladly and willingly.

Imagine how relieved and joyful Naomi and Ruth felt when they learned that Boaz had freed them from the misery of poverty and powerlessness. Theirs is only a fraction of the relief and joy Jesus brings to you as your willing and able Kinsman-Redeemer today!

Lord Jesus, as Your Spirit brings me awareness of my faults, let Him also grant me sure and firm belief in the freedom from guilt that You sacrificed Your life to buy for me. Relieved of guilt, I rejoice in the peace that comes only through faith in You. Amen.

The Way It's Done

*This was the custom in former times in Israel concerning
redeeming and exchanging: to confirm a transaction,
the one drew off his sandal and gave it to the other,
and this was the manner of attesting in Israel.*

RUTH 4:7 ESV

For many of us, learning about other cultures and traditions is the best part of travel. We like to get a glimpse into the everyday lives of those whose customs are different from our own, and we return home brimming with stories and observations.

If we could go back in time and hear Naomi's near-kinsman refuse to buy Elimelech's field, we would watch him take off his sandal and hand it to Boaz as a sign of his decision. His action in front of the called witnesses and gathered spectators sealed the deal. Although an unusual gesture from our point of view, it was meaningful to the Israelites of that time and place.

Just for fun, imagine if Ruth were to travel through the centuries and learn about our traditions! The children's egg hunt in a newly bloomed garden at Easter time; caps and gowns and speeches at the end of the school term; lavish fireworks displays in July; decorated wreaths and pine trees in homes every December. She would have plenty to tell Naomi when she returned home, wouldn't she?

Yet if we could overhear her, we would begin to realize how

similar we really are. We all have the same need to eat and sleep and find shelter. We all delight in music and dance, celebrations and festivities. And all of us living in community have found ways to reach mutual agreements, make binding contracts, and live in harmony with one another. The beauty of it lies in the many and various ways we go about these things!

Similarly, how we worship Jesus Christ differs among believers. Some of us find great meaning in the ancient chants and hymns of God's people and derive a deep sense of peace as we enter a centuries-old sanctuary. Others delight in modern anthems, spontaneous movement, and unfettered exclamations of praise. Still others bask in God's presence as they listen to His Word spoken in a natural setting, outdoors, with the breeze carrying the songs of their hearts to the skies.

How do you worship Jesus Christ? How do your traditions support your growth in His Spirit? Are there "new" traditions that would add to your joy in offering Him thanks and praise? What would help you find more joy in the blessings He has for you as you join with others in His name?

Lord Jesus, thank You for the many worship traditions that bring Your Word to Your people and turn our hearts to You. Show me how I can bring more joy to my own worship experience and better receive the blessings You have in store for me as I praise You. Amen.

Privileged Living

When the redeemer said to Boaz,
"Buy it for yourself," he drew off his sandal.

RUTH 4:8 ESV

The fellow made his decision. Because he could see only the responsibility involved and remained blind to the privilege, he wanted nothing to do with being Naomi's kinsman-redeemer. Boaz was welcome to it, and off came the man's sandal to emphasize the point.

In our lives too responsibilities can loom so large that we don't see the privileges attached to them. Say we're raising children and we get caught up in the day-to-day activities, appointments, errands, and obligations to the point that we lose sight of the tremendous honor that is ours. God has entrusted us with the care and nurturing of these little ones. We're the ones who receive their hugs and kisses, love and honor. No one else can take our privileged place in their hearts.

In the same way, any God-sent position of responsibility comes with its unique privileges. Are you caring for a sick spouse, needy relative, or elderly parent? Yes, there may be days when you wish you could put *on* your sandals and walk out! But you don't because God has given you the privilege of showing selfless and sacrificial love. When you can glimpse His plan for you, suddenly your responsibilities seem very small indeed.

Paid work as well as volunteer work come with both

responsibility and privilege too. With the responsibility of being dependable and carrying out certain tasks is the privilege of earning rewards (tangible or intangible); gaining self-confidence; acquiring experience; producing results; and receiving appreciation from others. But if we focus solely on our responsibilities, they become onerous and burdensome. Yet if we focus solely on our privileges, we become puffed up with our own importance. A clear vision of both gives us what God intends for us—willingness to give of ourselves to others and to our work; and an equal willingness to receive the lasting joy that our many privileges bring.

How do you feel about the responsibilities you have now? If one in particular seems burdensome to you, take time today to list at least one privilege you enjoy because this obligation is yours. Is it monetary? Then remind yourself where your money is going— food, clothing, shelter, recreation. You have the privilege of providing for others with your financial resources. Perhaps there's no money involved, but you have the responsibility of meeting certain God-sent obligations. You have the privilege of doing what's right in the sight of God. If you have responsibilities, you are living a privileged life!

Dear God, when my responsibilities threaten to overwhelm me, grant me the ability to see and appreciate the many privileges You continue to shower on me. In You I have the strength and power to do all my God-given tasks, and in You I have my true reward. Amen.

His Witnesses

Boaz told the town leaders and everyone else:
All of you are witnesses that today I have bought from
Naomi the property that belonged to Elimelech and
his two sons, Chilion and Mahlon.

RUTH 4:9 CEV

*P*icture the scene. Ten elders whispering among themselves as they consider all points of law and custom. Various townspeople gathered around, straining to hear every word of the proceedings. Then Boaz rises to speak. Silence! Who would want to miss what he would say? What they were about to hear would determine land ownership for generations to come. At last they would find out who would support the two destitute women in their midst, Naomi and Ruth. They were witnesses!

No doubt you have witnessed significant events in the lives of your friends and loved ones—graduations, marriages, birthdays, anniversaries. Perhaps you have witnessed an incident that made national or world news. What happened? What did you see? What did you hear? Those questions aren't asked by people interested in the comments of someone who, like them, knows about it only by hearsay or public announcement. They want to get your perspective because you were there and you saw it.

When others ask you about your faith, they're not looking for a scholarly commentary on the Bible or a debate about the fine points of religious practice. They can get that from theologically trained ministers and from books on the subject. What they want to know from you is how God has worked and is working in your life. They want to hear an authentic, personal, and truthful account, complete with real-life—your life!—examples. What have you witnessed?

You may never have seen a miraculous healing, but you may have felt the comfort of His presence during a time of illness, struggle, or grief. You might not be able to talk about a dramatic rescue, and you may never have laid eyes on an angel, but you can tell about the time you were afraid and His strength gave you confidence. There was the time you were stranded and a stranger appeared to help you and then vanished before you could thank him. There was the time you were confused and indecisive, and suddenly you remembered a certain Bible passage or what a particular pastor said, and you knew exactly what to do.

Whether you are just starting out on your spiritual journey with God or you have been His follower for many years, you are His witness. You have heard His promises and experienced His work in your life. To anyone who asks, tell what you know.

Lord Jesus, thank You for opening my heart and soul to
Your work in my life. Enable me to say, in my own words,
what You have done for me and the ways You have
blessed me. Grant me the willingness and courage
to tell what I know about You. Amen.

Essential Needs

"Also Ruth the Moabite, the widow of Mahlon, I have bought to be my wife, to perpetuate the name of the dead in his inheritance, that the name of the dead may not be cut off from among his brothers and from the gate of his native place. You are witnesses this day."

RUTH 4:10 ESV

*P*ublically, Boaz declared his intention to marry Ruth and sire children. It isn't far-fetched to think that this part of the transaction drew gasps of surprise from many onlookers! Certainly they admired Boaz for stepping forward to redeem Naomi's land. They knew that Boaz dealt honestly and would offer Naomi a fair price for the property. But marry Ruth, the Moabite? Have children by her so there would be a rightful heir to the property and Elimelech's name carried forward? That went far beyond the call of duty!

While money would take care of Naomi's material needs, it could never meet her spiritual needs. Land handed down through the generations ensured the perpetuation of one's name. After Elimelech died, the property became his sons'; but after they died, the only way a son could inherit the land would be if a relative married Ruth or Orpah and sired a son in Chilion or Mahlon's name. Naomi held out no hope that an Israelite would consent to do this for either of her Moabite daughters-in-law. That's why she had urged them both to return to their families rather than follow her to Bethlehem. But now a whole new situation presented itself. Boaz would marry Ruth and raise a son in Elimelech's name. Her kinsman-redeemer understood her grief, and now he would turn her tears to joy.

Again, Boaz illustrates how God meets essential needs. Sure, He provides you with what you need today—your food and water, clothing and shelter—according to His wisdom. Yet you have needs far more critical, and that's nourishment and refreshment for your soul. Because He understands your deepest grief, He does more than forgive you; He wraps you in the pure garments His Son Jesus earned for you. God, like Boaz, is willing to go beyond the call of duty so you can have everything you need to believe in Him and rest at ease in the abundance of His grace.

As Boaz did for Naomi, as God does for you, His Spirit stirs you to "go beyond the call of duty" for others. Look and see, listen and hear, so you understand more than their material needs. Give what no amount of money can buy, and that's your love.

Grant me, Lord Jesus, eyes to see and ears to hear the invisible, unspoken but essential needs of the ones I love. Along with doing all I can to alleviate material want, make me willing to provide their most important needs—friendship, encouragement, and the certainty that someone cares. Amen.

Win Over Worry

"Don't let this throw you.
You trust God, don't you? Trust me."

John 14:1 msg

Boaz had taken Naomi and Ruth's problems upon himself. He alone had the power and authority to lift them out of poverty and provide an heir to carry on the family name. Because of Boaz's outstanding reputation, they had every reason to believe he would keep his promises, and had no reason to worry.

But what if they had worried anyway? Suppose they thought, *What if Boaz has forgotten a legal point that will later invalidate the agreement? What if Boaz changes his mind or delays the marriage indefinitely or another woman claims his affections? What if Ruth proves unable to conceive a child? What if? What if?*

Worry on Naomi and Ruth's part simply would have pointed to one thing—lack of trust in Boaz. Worries about the legality of the transaction would have shown that they doubted his knowledge and authority. Worry about his commitment to Ruth would have revealed that they questioned his honesty, character, and integrity. Worry about Ruth's ability to conceive would have found them fretting over something beyond their control.

God urges us to give our worries, concerns, and anxieties to Him. He invites us to rely on His promise to remain with us, to strengthen us, to bring us through even the most trying circumstances, and to work everything according to His wisdom. Yet the more "what ifs" we entertain, the less we trust Him to follow through on His promises. Our worries question whether God knows what He's doing and truly has our best interests at heart. They imply that there are forces at work in the world that are more powerful than our all-powerful God. They tell God, despite His promise to be with us always, that we think He might abandon us sometime next week, next month, next year.

Today, take your worries to God. In your mind's eye, kneel at His feet and spread them out in front of Him, no matter how big or small they happen to be, or how significant or insignificant they are compared with the world's great problems. If you are worried about it, it's a problem for you. Hear the Lord speak, listen to His comforting words, and free your mind and heart to fully embrace His promises to you. And then stand up, thank Him, and walk away, and most importantly, leave all those worries behind. Win over worries by showing that you trust Him completely.

Shield me, Lord Jesus, from worry that casts doubt
on Your willingness and ability to fulfill Your promises.
My past, present, and future are in Your hands! Through
Your Spirit active in my heart, enable me to embrace Your
Word wholeheartedly and trust in You completely. Amen.

A Perfect Match

Charm is deceptive, and beauty does not last;
but a woman who fears the LORD will be greatly praised.

PROVERBS 31:30 NLT

They made an unlikely couple! Boaz: prosperous middle-aged landowner; born to a prominent Israelite family; and instructed from childhood in the laws and commandments of God, taught the history of God's presence among His people, and raised to revere the patriarchs of Israel. Ruth: penniless young widow; born into an ordinary Moabite family; and brought up to worship man-made deities in a culture rife with immorality and decadence. Are these two people compatible? We might say, "Probably no."

But God said, "Certainly yes." Ruth's faith in Naomi's God brought her into His household. By faith, she was as much a child of Abraham as was Boaz. The goodness that God's Spirit worked in her heart flowered in the compassion she showed Naomi, her commitment to the sorrowing woman, and her willingness to accept humble work to feed them both. Ruth's spiritual maturity led her to appreciate Boaz's character and integrity rather than set her heart on a less principled but more physically attractive suitor.

Boaz too allowed God's Spirit to lead him. Rather than condemn Ruth because of her heathen beginnings, he admired her for her faith, evidenced in how she acted. Instead of ogling freshly rouged faces and seductively smiling lips of other young women, Boaz looked beyond the dirt and grime of the fields that covered

Ruth's face and discovered a genuinely beautiful woman. A perfect match!

God is a master matchmaker. Many of us don't see ourselves as able, qualified, or worthy of playing any part in His great plans, but He sees us differently. Through Jesus' sacrifice on the cross, God cleanses us from sin and guilt. With His spiritual gifts of hope, peace, joy, and love, He lifts us out of spiritual poverty. Out of tender compassion, God brings us into His family, makes us fit for His work, and blesses us with everything we need to fulfill His plan for us. So we can put His love in action, He pours on us humility, kindness, selflessness, gentleness, and self-control. He supplies us with genuine, lasting, soul-deep beauty.

As you grow closer to Him, marvel at how what you bring from the past—your experience, knowledge, insight—matches what you need to meet today's challenges and help, encourage, or comfort someone right now. He matches the work He calls you to do with your qualities and capabilities. If you think you're lacking in anything, ask for it! You will get what you need because as a matchmaker, God doesn't make mistakes.

Dear God, so often I feel inferior to those around me who seem so spiritually advanced and well practiced in following Your ways. Grant me eyes to see myself as You see me— a member of Your family, qualified through the gifts of Your Spirit and rich in Your abundant blessings. Amen.

Meaningful Reward

All the people who were at the gate,
and the elders, said, "We are witnesses."

RUTH 4:11 NKJV

*B*oaz's marriage announcement brought loud cheers of approval. The crowd was on the verge of showering him and his wife-to-be with three magnificent blessings, each one uttered in the Lord God's holy name. Their blessings would mean more than any wedding gift that money could buy.

Few of our Spirit-inspired actions are played out in public or receive the applause of an adoring audience. Most, in fact, take place at home, in the workplace, in stores where we shop, or in parks where we take the children to play. It's among our family and friends that we have real opportunities to speak gently, listen carefully, and offer practical help. They're unlikely to heap praise on us every time we do them a good turn, and they may even forget to thank us.

Yes, sometimes our Spirit-motivated acts seem to pass by, barely noticed by those around us. How much more rewarding it would be to follow God's way of kindness, holiness, forgiveness, and compassion if only we heard more thanks, more praise, and more recognition of our spiritual lifestyle. The time we scratched from our calendar something we wanted to do and put in its place a loved one's preference or said no to temptation that tested our resolve to remain faithful, honest, true to our word—no one saw us do it. It's possible that we never told anyone what we did and never will. But if we think there wasn't a witness, we are mistaken. There was and always is a witness, and that witness is God.

He is the One you can depend on to see, approve, and encourage you as you continue to walk in His way. If the Spirit-inspired step you took is a tiny one, He will use it to make your next step a little bigger, and the one after that bigger yet. If the Spirit-supported decision you made was a big one—even a life-changing decision, as Ruth's decision to stay with Naomi and Boaz's decision to marry Ruth—He will be there to direct your path and give you all you need to continue on the way He has planned for you.

Although Boaz received a round of applause for doing what's right, he didn't need it. He would have taken the same course of action anyway. And so can you. Sometimes people will see your goodness and compliment you for it; great! But if they don't, that's okay too. God sees, and He blesses, and that's the best reward of all.

Dear God, You see everything that happens. Let my confidence in Your presence encourage me to continue in Your way and assure me that when I am doing what's right, I am acting according to Your will and pleasure. Grant me the blessings of confidence and strength. Amen.

First Blessing

*"May the LORD make this woman who is coming
into your home like Rachel and Leah, from whom
all the nation of Israel descended!"*

RUTH 4:11 NLT

She's one of us!" The crowd's cry of approval lifted Ruth from shunned foreigner to embraced family member. Though she had slipped into Bethlehem as a poverty-stricken stranger, she would now enter Boaz's home as a prosperous wife and God willing, become the mother of many children. How many? Rachel and Leah bore the revered patriarch Jacob twelve sons and one daughter, and from those twelve sons and their families emerged the twelve tribes of Israel. Their first blessing embraced Ruth as an honored mother of Israel: "And now may she bear an abundance of children! Let them laugh and play in the streets of Bethlehem!"

Jesus has brought you into His family, God's family. The Holy Spirit has opened the door for you by creating faith in your heart. Come in! As you sit in His presence and hear Him speak through the words of scripture, imagine you are visiting a revered elder. His conversation reminds you of all that God has done in the lives of His people throughout history, and highlights His promises to you today. Your trust in Him deepens the longer you listen. Faith gets stronger and more alive.

The Spirit speaks of all that Jesus has done for you so you can have a family relationship with Him, addressing His Father in heaven as your Father in heaven. Your gratitude for His willingness to win this great prize for you increases every time you reflect on it. Faith gets richer. Yet faith won't remain hidden in your heart, silent, and unproductive. Faith longs to come out and play. You want it to!

Loving parents delight in seeing their children romp, laugh, shout, work, and play in the real world. Even though there will be stumbles and even a few scars, that's the only way children can learn and grow, make progress and gain confidence. Similarly, the rough-and-tumble everyday world is where your faith develops too. It's the only place you can practice God's teachings, put God's promises to the test, learn what you're able to do because of your faith, and discover your spiritual strengths and weaknesses.

Let your faith bear an abundance of positive thoughts, encouraging words, and self-giving actions. When God's Spirit stirs you to do a small kindness today, do it, even if—maybe especially if—it's something you wouldn't naturally do. Let your faith come out and play today!

Heavenly Father, thank You for the faith You have planted in me. Enable me to let it grow, nurtured by Your Spirit as it becomes evident in the things I do and say every day and in common, ordinary situations. Enliven me, strengthen me, nourish me in Your love. Amen.

Second Blessing

May you be a rich man in the tribe of
Ephrath and an important man in Bethlehem.

RUTH 4:11 CEV

o right-thinking person hopes for disaster to strike! The crowd's second blessing wished Boaz increased material wealth and the continuance of his godly reputation and honored status in the community. Their words reflected the desire of any person of goodwill, that tangible resources and intangible assets would grow and increase.

Yet there's an added element to the Bethlehemites' words that make them more than simple good wishes from well-meaning friends. "May the Lord do this!" opened the blessing they conferred on Boaz and Ruth, and to the Lord they offered their prayers for the couple. As believers in the one true God, they understood that all good things come from His hand. They wished the best for Boaz and Ruth but didn't presume that they knew, as God knows, what is best in the lives of His people.

Gathered at the gate of Bethlehem, they were thinking of Boaz's financial prosperity when they mentioned riches, but they were well aware that God's riches include strength born of adversity, confidence bolstered by challenges, and character built by temptations faced and conquered. Those are great riches! While the crowd celebrated Boaz's leadership and fame, they also knew that others among them were equal to him in fairness, godliness, compassion, and generosity. Maybe one of the least-noticed men or women in Bethlehem even surpassed him—who knows the real reputation of a person but God alone?

In the name of your good and gracious Lord Jesus, pray that He will bless you and your loved ones. Yes, describe what you most desire: good health, financial stability, rewarding relationships, productive opportunities, increasing success. Tell Him you want others to notice you, to like you, to speak well of you, and to count you as a valued friend.

And then bless Him. Bless Him by thanking Him for inviting you to pray and for the peace of mind you receive by entrusting Him with your needs and desires. Praise Him for the way He works in the lives of people, even when His ways are mysterious and His wisdom incomprehensible to us. Worship Him because He is your Creator and Protector, Shepherd and Friend. He is your God!

Pray to Him for all the wonderful things life has to offer. Pray for yourself and for others. Pray in His name, knowing and believing that He knows and gives what is best for each of us.

Lord Jesus, I pray that You would bless me with everything I need for my physical well-being, according to Your good will. Pour on me the spiritual riches You promise all who come to You so I may possess true wealth and an honorable reputation in Your eyes. Amen.

Third Blessing

*"Through the offspring the LORD gives you by this
young woman, may your family be like that of
Perez, whom Tamar bore to Judah."*

RUTH 4:12 NIV

I n the Lord's name," the people concluded, "may your children
be a credit to you and bring praise to your family for many
generations to come!"

This final blessing highlights the love and respect Ruth had
earned among the people of Bethlehem. They elevated her to the
level of Tamar, the mother of Perez, who was the son of Judah and
ancestor of Boaz, of the tribe of Judah.

It could not have been far from their minds that the patriarch Judah had married a Canaanite woman, a nonIsraelite, with
whom he had three sons. His first son married Tamar, likely also a
Canaanite. Upon the death of her husband and without children,
Tamar went to his brother, who had the duty of begetting a son
by her to carry his elder brother's name. But this second son was
unwilling to sire a child for his brother. When the second son died,
Judah advised Tamar to go back to her family, and later she could
marry his third son.

Time made it clear, however, that Judah had no intention of
honoring his promise and his obligation. Furious at her father-in-
law's ill treatment of her, the inventive woman disguised herself as a
prostitute and invited him to spend the night with her. That is how

she became the mother of Perez, ancestor of Boaz, ancestor of King David, ancestor of Jesus Christ.

Tamar and Ruth were outcasts, but God gave both a special place in His family. In Bible times and today, He sometimes chooses the most unlikely people to serve Him, prepare His way, and play an important role in the history of His people. During their lifetimes, however, each person is simply doing what they must under the circumstances. God used Canaan-born Tamar's right to bear a child in the family to bring Perez into the world. He used Israel-born Naomi's desire to return to the land of her birth to bring Ruth to Bethlehem. He used Moab-born Ruth's need to get food to bring her into contact with Boaz; and He used Israel-born Boaz's honorable character to bring about his marriage with Ruth.

God's family includes you. What you do today to follow Him, to serve Him as His Spirit directs you, may seem small, ordinary, and not necessarily heroic. You are simply responding to your circumstances and meeting your needs and the needs of others. But in His family, you never know how you might be fitting into His plans!

---

*Heavenly Father, thank You for showing me how
You use each of us to fulfill Your purposes in the world.
Grant that what I do may inspire others, even those who
come after me, to commit their lives to You, no matter
who they are or how others see them. Amen.*

Unlimited God

"With God all things are possible."

MATTHEW 19:26 NKJV

*N*aomi and Ruth's days of need were over. From now on, they would have more than enough, yet even in the household of wealthy and generous Boaz, there were limits. He possessed a finite sum of money, a measurable inventory of household goods, a certain number of fields, and a precise number of head of cattle.

In our relationship with God through Christ, however, there are no limits. His love and compassion don't come with boundaries we dare not overstep. He never measures the mercy He pours on us, stopping when we've received our fair share. That would be impossible because His mercy is without end for everybody. He isn't counting the number of times He forgives us but forgives every repentant heart that comes to Him, every time.

The limits rest with us. Our time, abilities, and opportunities are limited. There are limits to our patience and endurance, willingness to forgive and power to love. There's a limit to what we can buy, use, share, give, and keep. There's a limit to what we can expect of ourselves and expect of others, and we invite trouble if we overstep those boundaries.

These are limits we live with every day, so it's no wonder we apply to God those things we know about ourselves and our world. We have trouble remembering that God lives outside time, and His capacities defy human understanding. How many times have we cried in exasperation, "I can't be in two places at once!" But God can be in all places at once. He is everywhere.

Why place restrictions on what He can do for you by praying for less than what your heart desires? Though He has given you many blessings, why step back when He wants to give you more? Are you afraid that He doesn't know what He's doing or He's going to run out of good things for others?

Your Heavenly Father, who created you, has enough love to last you now through eternity. Delight in His presence, and relax in His peace. His Son Jesus, who died and rose again to win your salvation, has forgiveness to offer for every little (and not so little) sin. Ask for His mercy as many times as you like. His Holy Spirit, who opens the way of God to you, has more than you can imagine to show you. Walk with Him wherever He takes you, as slowly as He takes you or as quickly as He takes you. Grow in faith and hope, generosity and compassion without stopping to measure because when you limit God, you only limit yourself.

Lord God, Your love, might, and holiness are beyond my understanding. Grant me the faith it takes to come before You with all my needs and dreams, asking You to fulfill them according to Your will. Let me never limit You by limiting what I think You can do! Amen.

PART 4:

Boaz Marries Ruth

Happy Change

Boaz took Ruth, and she became his wife.

RUTH 4:13 ESV

t the beginning of spring harvest, Ruth entered Boaz's gate as nothing more than an indigent foreigner scavenging for food. Shortly after the end of the harvest, she walked into his house as Boaz's wife, a woman fully embraced by the community and one of their own. What a happy change!

In your own life, no doubt you have experienced many happy changes. You might recall a time when you moved into a new neighborhood, joined a new group, or hired on at a new workplace. On day one, you didn't know a soul. Then, after only a short time had passed, you learned people's names and they learned yours. Friendships formed, and you no longer felt unsure, lonely, or uncomfortable. God blessed you with a very happy change.

How many times have you heard or made remarks like these: "Only three years ago, we were deep in debt; but this month we paid off our last loan and even have a savings account!" "This time last spring, you were just coming out of surgery, but look how healthy you are now!" "A week ago, there was no end in sight, but today a real opportunity has opened up for me!"

Sometimes we resist change because it takes us from familiar surroundings to unfamiliar, from people who know us well to people we've never met. Change isn't easy for most of us, often to the point that we hesitate to change from difficulties that we do know to more favorable circumstances that we don't know!

Let God lead you through life's changes. The less you fear change, the more happiness you will find in all circumstances. Embrace the change He brings, even if it's a change you didn't initiate and perhaps did not welcome. But it's possible that this is the very change He will use to show you how strong and capable you really are; to build your knowledge, experience, and confidence so you can more fully enjoy life; to increase your spiritual insight and wisdom, which will bring you lasting contentment and peace of mind. You can never fully possess these gifts if nothing ever changes!

Today, think about the happy changes that have taken place over the past year or five years or ten years. You have grown in mind and heart. You know more than you did then, and you have many reasons to celebrate. Let God make every change a happy change for you.

Dear God, open my mind and heart to the changes that take place in my life. Grant me the courage to accept them without fear and find in them the blessings You have in store for me. Let every season of my life, Lord, bring me closer to You. Amen.

PART 5:

The Genealogy of David

Gift of Life

*He went in to her, and the LORD gave
her conception, and she bore a son.*

RUTH 4:13 ESV

The writer of Ruth emphasizes a point many of us forget: God is the giver of life. When we reflect on this truth, our view of life itself changes in three essential ways.

First, our perception of life becomes clearer when we recognize God as the source of it and that He created us in His own image. We're compelled to accept not just ourselves but everyone else as one of God's in-His-own-image creations. No matter where a person comes from, what he looks like, who society says she is, God gave life to him or her. This is the same God who breathed the breath of life into Adam and Eve, Naomi and Ruth and Boaz, all the believers throughout the ages, and each one of us today. When we look in the eyes of others, when we look in the mirror, we're seeing someone God created. How could we, then, use words that cause unnecessary pain or make comments that are needlessly unkind?

Second, our view of our own lives can't help but become more positive when we believe God is the author of it. This great truth provides the best and surest foundation for strong self-esteem—God does not create shoddy merchandise! Why listen to negative self-talk? Why harbor doubts about worthiness or importance in the world? Because God made each one of us, we can take on life with reality-based self-confidence and a positive self-image.

Third, in seeing life as God-created and positive, life becomes meaningful. We look to God for our purpose, and we discover it through the guidance of His Holy Spirit and our God-given abilities and opportunities. We can no longer think that life belongs to us and we can waste it or spend it at will. Nor can we believe that the sole purpose of life is to look out for number one. Unless we look to God who gave us life for the meaning of life, we'll never find it.

Just for a moment, stand in the shoes of someone who believes that human life is not God-given. How would this kind of thinking affect your self-perception, your behavior, your goals, your relationships? What would you conclude is the meaning of life? What would you say about birth, about death?

Now put your own shoes back on. In your mind's eye, watch God creating you, and see His eyes soften with love. Breathe deeply, filling yourself with His presence. How do you feel about yourself now? Good—because He has a divine purpose for you!

Creator-God, thank You for the gift of life. Forgive
me for the times I have placed little worth on myself
and for those times I have done or said something to
diminish another person's life. Grant me eyes to see
You in the faces of everyone I meet. Amen.

Woo-hoo for You!

After his birth, the women said to Naomi:
Praise the LORD! Today he has given you a grandson
to take care of you. We pray that the boy will grow
up to be famous everywhere in Israel.

RUTH 4:14 CEV

The baby captured Naomi's heart! You can imagine how her eyes filled with tears to look at this new little life added to the family of Elimelech. Naomi must have longed to share with her beloved husband, gone these many seasons, this happy news—a son had been born, a son who belonged to him. This boy was now the owner of his grandfather's property, the land that had been in their family for generations. God willing, descendants would follow, and the name of Elimelech would remain forever in the town of Bethlehem.

Yes, once again, Naomi was the talk of the town. Only a year earlier, the townswomen had pitied her, but now they showered her with exclamations of joy. Where they had shaken their heads to consider how much she had lost, now they clapped their hands to celebrate all she had gained. Naomi, the very woman who had described herself as empty not too long ago was now full—full of hope, full of joy, full of love.

You know what it feels like to be the center of attention. Say it's your birthday, and all your friends shower you with cards and gifts and cheer as you blow out the candles on your cake. Or maybe it's the day you graduate, marry, or celebrate the life of a loved one. Your friends and loved ones pay attention to you, letting you know they are there for you.

But have you ever thought about how important you are to them? You share in their most important celebrations. Yours is the voice of their praises and the touch of their comfort in times of grief. Their special times are your opportunities to acknowledge their milestones, achievements, and successes. When they go through hard times, your presence lets them know that you care enough to be there with them and for them.

Yes, you're a familiar face in their world, and their faces are regulars in your world. It's easy to take one another for granted! Yet when there's something to celebrate, an event to commemorate, a milestone to mark, aren't you glad they are there with you? And that's the gift you give them when you can say, "I'm here for you." You can clap your hands together and shout along with the women who filled Naomi's home, "Woo-hoo for you!"

Thank You, Lord God, for those who share my good times, mark my milestones, and comfort me in times of sadness. Let all these dear ones remind me that my presence in their lives is a way of serving You as I show how much I care for them. Amen.

Real Relationships

"May he restore your youth
and care for you in your old age."

RUTH 4:15 NLT

Every Israelite family prayed for a son, and now Naomi's prayer had been answered. In Bible times, and still in many cultures today, adult children were responsible for their aged and disabled family members. Except in rare cases, men inherited land and controlled the majority of wealth, so a male child meant security for the future. Fathers depended on sons to take over the family land or business when they were too frail to continue, and to provide for them and the women in the household.

Ideally, the eldest son willingly took on his responsibility and saw to his parents' material and emotional well-being. Again, ideally, both adult sons and daughters looked to their elders as a source of wisdom, and valued them as their link to the generations that went before them. The bonds of love and duty drew people together in families where each member found support, stability, security, and faithful companionship.

But then as now, few relationships are ideal. Within our families and our circle of friends, disputes arise, misunderstandings occur, and obligations are sometimes unmet. If we lack the willingness to mend the inevitable rifts, our relationships disintegrate. While we might justify inaction on our hope to prove a point, exact revenge, or teach a lesson, we're deceiving ourselves. With each relationship we discard for frivolous, emotional, or self-centered reasons, we diminish our future.

God gives you relationships to enhance your life. Your family and friends are there to help and encourage you, share the good times with you, and be there for you when times are rough. He has put you in their lives for the same reason. Many of the relationships you enjoy today are also your security for the future. In them, you will have people around you who know you better than anyone else—your dreams and achievements, your likes and dislikes, your inmost thoughts and feelings. And you for them because you've been through so much together. No one else, no matter how important in your life later, can ever take their place in your heart; and the same is true about your place in their hearts.

Ask God for the willingness to forgive and to mend rifts while you can. Ask Him for the strength to overcome less-than-ideal situations and the wisdom to cherish relationships despite the rough spots. Let Him make you the one who knows how much relationships mean today and will mean through every tomorrow. Make the future brighter, richer, and more secure for all of you.

Dear God, thank You for those who mean so much to me.
Help me do my part to keep our relationship open,
healthy, enriching, and joyful for all of us. Let me not
focus on ideal relationships but on real ones for my
present happiness and future fulfillment. Amen.

Have Everything!

*"He is the son of your daughter-in-law who loves
you and has been better to you than seven sons!"*

RUTH 4:15 NLT

What a compliment to Ruth! In a culture where sons were every woman's hope, Naomi's friends and relatives made an astute observation. Yes, the mother of sons had status in the community, and the security of having someone to take care of her in her later years. But there was something even more lasting, more worthwhile, more to be desired, and that was what Ruth gave Naomi—voluntary, genuine love. Love played out in word and action. Ruth's love was more valuable than the love even seven sons could give her!

Ruth's love, multiplied an infinite number of times, is the love God has for you. His love is voluntary on His part and genuine. He is the source of all love, and not even a fraction of His love is tainted by selfish motives or hidden intentions.

God gives His love even when we don't deserve it. After our fall into sin, God had no need or obligation to love us. Few of us, after seeing a once-loved vase shattered into a million minute particles, would continue to keep that vase. Instead, we'd sweep up the pieces and throw them away. But God chose not to do that. Although sin left us unidentifiable as God's-image perfect, God still loved us. God chose to keep us.

His love is played out in word and action. He spoke His

promise to send a Savior and fulfilled it when He sent His Son Jesus into our world. Through Jesus, our Heavenly Father put His compassion into action by healing those sick in body and those suffering in soul; curing those blind in the eyes and those sightless in spirit; and raising those dead in the tomb and those dead in their sins.

We cherish the love that others give us because their love means more than words can say. We can't imagine life without it! But without God's love, we couldn't have life at all. He gives us His Spirit to enliven faith and fill us with His wisdom, so we can experience His spiritual gifts and glimpse the things of God. Through the promise of a Savior and its fulfillment in Jesus, He created a living, loving relationship between us and Himself. With Jesus as our example, He shows us how to love and makes it possible for us to share His love with others. His love is worth everything.

You have God's love. Delight in it and give thanks because now you have everything and have everything to give!

God of love, You are the Source of all love. Invite me to embrace Your love with my whole heart, filling my soul and spirit with the certainty of Your mercy, grace, and compassion. Endow me with the willingness and ability to love others as You love me. Amen.

New Life

Naomi took the child in her arms and cared for him.

RUTH 4:16 NIV

*a*t her lowest point, Naomi had given up on life. With her husband and sons gone, she returned to Bethlehem a broken woman. Her only option, as she saw it, was to sell the family property and wait for death.

But with the new life born to Ruth and Boaz came Naomi's rebirth. From the depths of sorrow, God raised her to the heights of joy, purpose, and hope for the future. In her old age, God blessed her with new life.

Disappointment and loss, advanced age and serious illness—many of life's difficult circumstances can make a person wonder if there's anything left, any good reason to keep on living. You've heard the cries: "I'll never love again!" "I'll never get back to the way I was!" "I'll never have a job anything like the one I had before!" "Without him, I really don't want to go on." Perhaps similar words crossed your lips at one time.

What happened? You wept and you prayed. In your weakness, you leaned on His strength, and even without your knowing exactly when, you learned to accept what had happened and found peace within your heart. For the first time in a long time, you began to notice a few things that made you smile—a child's voice; an amusing anecdote; a welcome invitation; a caring friend; a budding flower. You saw an opportunity to help someone, and you took it. That led to a new friendship, a fresh start, a surprising ability, a rebirth of interest, a new reason to go on living.

Have you ever lain awake in the predawn hours, impatient for the day to begin? The more times you looked at the clock, the slower the minutes passed. The more you focused on the darkness, the darker it grew. You thought morning would never come, but of course it did. And when the alarm sounded, you wondered why you passed up your chance to sleep when you could!

Similarly, there may come times of darkness in your life. It might appear as a night of change, reevaluation, reprioritizing, or pulling in. You might go through a time of trial, temptation, or spiritual dryness. But give up on life? Never! God will send a new season, a new day. He has plans for you—the new you, wiser, more experienced, and more thoughtful than before. And you are ready to be blessed with a new life in Him.

God creates hope in the heart that trusts in Him. Let Him do that for you today.

Heavenly Father, enable me to put my trust in You. Restore me with strength for today and hope for the future. Let me rest easy until You bring the light of day into my heart, and then let me thank and praise You for the gift of my new life. Amen.

One Who Serves

*The neighborhood women named him Obed,
but they called him "Naomi's Boy."*

RUTH 4:17 CEV

Obed means "one who serves." His birth established him as rightful heir to the land that would have belonged to Ruth's deceased husband, Mahlon. The day Obed was born, he served as the redeemer of this property. When he was grown, he was expected to serve as Naomi's protector, taking care of her in her last years.

Service wasn't all one-sided, however. Naomi would serve baby Obed as his caregiver, teaching him as he grew to know, love, and worship the God of Israel. She would instruct the boy in the history of his people, in God's dealings with them and His promises to them. She would tell Obed about the coming Messiah, pointing his young eyes upward to the things of heaven. And she would show him how to live on earth as a compassionate, honored, and honorable servant of all, like his father, Boaz. She would prepare him for his life of privileged service.

God calls you "one who serves." When faith was born in your heart, you were put in a position to follow Him by serving others as the compassionate one, the one who forgives, the one with the courage to stand up for what's true, fair, and right. Your rebirth in Him means you are to serve by giving generously, speaking thoughtfully, acting purposefully, and living joyfully. God expects it of you now that you faith has brought you into His family.

But your service, like Obed's, isn't all one-sided. If it were all up to you, your service would be nothing less than rules, regulations, and arduous duty! Instead, He lifts your eyes to the life of Jesus Christ, who, though King of kings, was born in a humble place to humble people. He came to serve and did so, even to the cross to show the seriousness of sin; then to the tomb to show the reality of sin; and then to His resurrection to show His victory over sin—a victory He won for you.

He serves you by comforting you when you grieve, picking you up when you stumble, renewing you when you come to Him, and loving you always. When you read or hear His Word, He teaches you about the history of your spiritual family, and you learn about how He has worked in the lives of His people. When you talk to your sisters and brothers in Christ, He helps you see how you can serve faithfully and well. Because He serves you, you experience both the privilege and the joy of being called "the one who serves."

Thank You, dear God, for renewing and nourishing me so I can better serve You through willing, humble service to others. Teach me the ways I can be of service, and keep me aware of those who are longing for someone to listen, care, and serve them in love. Amen.

Shepherd's Work

Obed was the father of Jesse, and Jesse the father of David.

RUTH 4:17 MSG

David rose to greatness in the history of Israel, surpassed only by Jesus, who descended from the line of David. David was Israel's second king after Saul. Strong, handsome, and gifted, David fought battles, worshipped the one true God, composed music, played the harp, and wrote poetry. He displayed compassion when he was given an opportunity to kill King Saul, the man who wanted to kill him, but succumbed to temptation when attracted to another man's wife, Bathsheba. In some ways, David was a forerunner of Christ; and in other ways, he was just like us in his need for forgiveness and redemption.

Born in Bethlehem the youngest of eight brothers, David was not considered "most likely to succeed." In normal circumstances, he would have lived out his life in the shadow of Jesse's other sons. The first son would inherit most of the property upon their father's death. Even if the eldest should die, six more brothers were ahead of David! Indeed, as a youngster, David was put in charge of his father's sheep.

Shepherding was a humble position. By day, shepherds led their flocks far out into the hills in search of good pastureland so their sheep could eat, and clear, still water for their sheep to drink. Before nightfall, shepherds gathered the animals together and coaxed them one by one into a sheepfold, a protected area.

To keep them safe from foxes and wolves, shepherds remained on watch throughout the hours of darkness.

Humble, ordinary, tedious, dull—but for David, a training ground for greatness. Out in the hills and miles from town, he learned courage and resourcefulness. He wouldn't have lasted for long if he didn't know how to instantly kill a predator with a well-aimed stone. He had to make do when supplies dwindled and emergencies arose. David learned the needs of his sheep and met them—and do sheep ever have needs! If their shepherd doesn't guide them to sources of food and water, sheep won't find them. If he won't go first along a narrow path, sheep won't take it. Sheep can't heal their own wounds, calm their own fears, or protect themselves from predators. Only their shepherd can. Later, David shepherded the people of Israel to the heights of glory and victory.

Today, Jesus shepherds you. Let Him guide you to the nourishment of His Good News of forgiveness and peace. Follow Him on the path He knows is best for you. Let Him heal and comfort you, protect and love you as only your Good Shepherd can.

Dear Jesus, my Good Shepherd, bring me into Your flock.
Be the Shepherd of my life, and let me follow wherever
You lead. Enable me to hear the sound of Your voice and
obey Your commands. Bring me into the shelter of
Your compassion, protection, and love. Amen.

Family Tree

This, then, is the family line of Perez: Perez was the father of Hezron. . .Salmon the father of Boaz, Boaz the father of Obed, Obed the father of Jesse, and Jesse the father of David.

Ruth 4:18, 21–22 niv

What a family tree! The writer of Ruth traces King David's lineage from Perez, a son of Judah. Judah was one of the twelve sons of Isaac, and Isaac was the son of Abraham. In the book of Genesis, there are two other genealogies that connect the great patriarch Abraham with our first parents, Adam and Eve. And it is to them that God promised a Savior.

Why a Savior? Because Adam and Eve, given free will by God, who created them, did what any of us would have done—they wanted more than what God had provided. They chose not to let God be God but wanted themselves to be God. "No more of this accepting God's say-so," they said. "Let's decide for ourselves what's best for us."

Human pride broke the perfect relationship that had existed between God and His creation. While He could have let the rift remain, He didn't. Instead, in the cool of the evening in the Garden of Eden, God made a promise. Through the miracle of human birth would come a Savior. This Savior, willing and able, would take upon Himself the sins of all people from Adam and Eve forward until the end of time. He would possess the power to atone for sin, to wipe away the stain of sin from all who have faith in Him. He would be the bridge to God for sinners who desire salvation.

Adam, Eve, Naomi, Ruth, Boaz, Obed, and King David—each looked forward in Spirit-planted faith to the promised Savior. Their faith in His coming led them to God's eternal kingdom. We look back in Spirit-planted faith to the One God has sent. Born in Bethlehem, just as the prophets said, Jesus fulfilled His Heavenly Father's divine promise. Our faith that His work on our behalf is effective and accepted by God leads us to His eternal kingdom.

Your family tree of faith includes illustrious names and humble names—names of those remembered down through the ages and names known to only a few and now lost to history. There are names you'd expect to be there and no doubt names that will surprise you, even startle you. Who knows the ways of faith, love, and His Holy Spirit? But right now, it's your name that counts. Come before your Heavenly Father because through the faith He has put in your heart, your name is on His family tree.

Heavenly Father, thank You for sending Your Son Jesus into the world so every repentant heart can receive the gift of salvation. Thank You for the promise You made so long ago and fulfilled at the right time; thank You for adding my name to Your family tree. Amen.

Chosen One

"You did not choose Me, but I chose you."

JOHN 15:16 NKJV

*G*od chose Ruth to play an important part in His plan of salvation. But that doesn't mean she was born with a halo over her head! Nor did there ever come the day in her life when she woke up and realized that her name would appear in the genealogies of King David and Jesus Christ. Hardly!

Growing up in an idol-worshipping culture, Ruth probably thought that the God of Israel was just another deity. When she married Mahlon and moved into the home he shared with his parents, his brother, and his brother's wife, it's possible that which god they worshipped mattered little to her. After all, who cared? But then she began to notice a difference in the lives of her husband, his brother, and her mother- and father-in-law. They behaved unlike their pleasure-seeking Moabite neighbors, and she was intrigued by what she saw.

During the day while the men worked in the fields and the women ground the grain, you could hear Naomi telling her Moabite daughters-in-law about the history of her people—descendants promised to the great patriarch Abraham, freedom sent to Israelites in Egypt, victories with the help of God's strength and might, a Messiah promised to the world. Naomi taught the young women God's commandments, given to His people on Mount Sinai. Ruth took in what Naomi told her and saw that

Naomi's actions matched her words.

Ruth and Orpah would have been obliged to sit quietly and respectfully as their Israelite family prayed, sang, and recalled God's words to them. But Ruth's eyes followed their every movement, her body visibly relaxed as she felt God's comfort, and her interest grew as she grasped the truth of God's compassion, love, protection, and care.

Ruth remained true to the faith God had worked in her heart. Day to day, she let Him nourish her soul, and soon her thoughts, words, and actions, like Naomi's, reflected His living presence. The more convinced of His love she became, the shallower, the sillier any other god looked to her. Why return to a man-made wooden idol when the true God was welcoming her with open arms? The longer her commitment, the stronger her determination to follow Him, wherever He would lead.

You are like Ruth. You do not know why God has chosen you or for what purpose, but He has chosen you. The growing, building, strengthening faith in your heart proves it! His commitment to you is sure. The only question remains: How far are you willing to go with your commitment to Him?

Almighty God, thank You for sending Your Spirit into my heart. Enable me to joyfully receive the faith You have planted in me, and let Your Spirit continue to feed, nourish, cultivate, and increase this faith so my thoughts, words, and actions conform to Your will. Amen.

In the Light of Ruth

What a journey! Ruth moved from one country to another; from a humble gleaner in the field to respected place in the household; and from scorned childlessness to honored motherhood.

Ruth's amazing journey began the same way yours does—with the faith that God's Spirit stirs in your heart. As you step forward with Him in faith, you discover new thoughts and a fresh way to perceive the world. His Spirit travels right along with you, so you're never alone.

Look around at your traveling companions. See Boaz and those like him today who apply God's guidelines to their everyday dealings. See Naomi and those like her today whose example draws others to God. See Ruth and those like her today who are willing to follow where God leads, even when there's nothing but unfamiliar territory ahead. Let them encourage you and remind you that you are not alone but among the family of God.

Keep traveling! You can't exhaust His willingness to receive, restore, and renew a sorrowing heart. No matter where you are on your spiritual journey, there's something new to delight in, discover, and savor. Your travels continue each time you say with Ruth, "Wherever You go, I will go." Embrace, experience, and enjoy your journey with Him.

Scripture Index

OLD TESTAMENT

NEW TESTAMENT

Read Through the
Bible in a Year

1-Jan	Gen. 1-2	Matt. 1	Ps. 1
2-Jan	Gen. 3-4	Matt. 2	Ps. 2
3-Jan	Gen. 5-7	Matt. 3	Ps. 3
4-Jan	Gen. 8-10	Matt. 4	Ps. 4
5-Jan	Gen. 11-13	Matt. 5:1-20	Ps. 5
6-Jan	Gen. 14-16	Matt. 5:21-48	Ps. 6
7-Jan	Gen. 17-18	Matt. 6:1-18	Ps. 7
8-Jan	Gen. 19-20	Matt. 6:19-34	Ps. 8
9-Jan	Gen. 21-23	Matt. 7:1-11	Ps. 9:1-8
10-Jan	Gen. 24	Matt. 7:12-29	Ps. 9:9-20
11-Jan	Gen. 25-26	Matt. 8:1-17	Ps. 10:1-11
12-Jan	Gen. 27:1-28:9	Matt. 8:18-34	Ps. 10:12-18
13-Jan	Gen. 28:10-29:35	Matt. 9	Ps. 11
14-Jan	Gen. 30:1-31:21	Matt. 10:1-15	Ps. 12
15-Jan	Gen. 31:22-32:21	Matt. 10:16-36	Ps. 13
16-Jan	Gen. 32:22-34:31	Matt. 10:37-11:6	Ps. 14
17-Jan	Gen. 35-36	Matt. 11:7-24	Ps. 15
18-Jan	Gen. 37-38	Matt. 11:25-30	Ps. 16
19-Jan	Gen. 39-40	Matt. 12:1-29	Ps. 17
20-Jan	Gen. 41	Matt. 12:30-50	Ps. 18:1-15
21-Jan	Gen. 42-43	Matt. 13:1-9	Ps. 18:16-29
22-Jan	Gen. 44-45	Matt. 13:10-23	Ps. 18:30-50
23-Jan	Gen. 46:1-47:26	Matt. 13:24-43	Ps. 19
24-Jan	Gen. 47:27-49:28	Matt. 13:44-58	Ps. 20
25-Jan	Gen. 49:29-Exod. 1:22	Matt. 14	Ps. 21
26-Jan	Exod. 2-3	Matt. 15:1-28	Ps. 22:1-21
27-Jan	Exod. 4:1-5:21	Matt. 15:29-16:12	Ps. 22:22-31
28-Jan	Exod. 5:22-7:24	Matt. 16:13-28	Ps. 23
29-Jan	Exod. 7:25-9:35	Matt. 17:1-9	Ps. 24
30-Jan	Exod. 10-11	Matt. 17:10-27	Ps. 25
31-Jan	Exod. 12	Matt. 18:1-20	Ps. 26
1-Feb	Exod. 13-14	Matt. 18:21-35	Ps. 27

2-Feb	Exod. 15-16	Matt. 19:1-15	Ps. 28
3-Feb	Exod. 17-19	Matt. 19:16-30	Ps. 29
4-Feb	Exod. 20-21	Matt. 20:1-19	Ps. 30
5-Feb	Exod. 22-23	Matt. 20:20-34	Ps. 31:1-8
6-Feb	Exod. 24-25	Matt. 21:1-27	Ps. 31:9-18
7-Feb	Exod 26-27	Matt. 21:28-46	Ps. 31:19-24
8-Feb	Exod. 28	Matt. 22	Ps. 32
9-Feb	Exod. 29	Matt. 23:1-36	Ps. 33:1-12
10-Feb	Exod. 30-31	Matt. 23:37-24:28	Ps. 33:13-22
11-Feb	Exod. 32-33	Matt. 24:29-51	Ps. 34:1-7
12-Feb	Exod. 34:1-35:29	Matt. 25:1-13	Ps. 34:8-22
13-Feb	Exod. 35:30-37:29	Matt. 25:14-30	Ps. 35:1-8
14-Feb	Exod. 38-39	Matt. 25:31-46	Ps. 35:9-17
15-Feb	Exod. 40	Matt. 26:1-35	Ps. 35:18-28
16-Feb	Lev. 1-3	Matt. 26:36-68	Ps. 36:1-6
17-Feb	Lev. 4:1-5:13	Matt. 26:69-27:26	Ps. 36:7-12
18-Feb	Lev. 5:14 -7:21	Matt. 27:27-50	Ps. 37:1-6
19-Feb	Lev. 7:22-8:36	Matt. 27:51-66	Ps. 37:7-26
20-Feb	Lev. 9-10	Matt. 28	Ps. 37:27-40
21-Feb	Lev. 11-12	Mark 1:1-28	Ps. 38
22-Feb	Lev. 13	Mark 1:29-39	Ps. 39
23-Feb	Lev. 14	Mark 1:40-2:12	Ps. 40:1-8
24-Feb	Lev. 15	Mark 2:13-3:35	Ps. 40:9-17
25-Feb	Lev. 16-17	Mark 4:1-20	Ps. 41:1-4
26-Feb	Lev. 18-19	Mark 4:21-41	Ps. 41:5-13
27-Feb	Lev. 20	Mark 5	Ps. 42-43
28-Feb	Lev. 21-22	Mark 6:1-13	Ps. 44
1-Mar	Lev. 23-24	Mark 6:14-29	Ps. 45:1-5
2-Mar	Lev. 25	Mark 6:30-56	Ps. 45:6-12
3-Mar	Lev. 26	Mark 7	Ps. 45:13-17
4-Mar	Lev. 27	Mark 8	Ps. 46
5-Mar	Num. 1-2	Mark 9:1-13	Ps. 47

6-Mar	Num. 3	Mark 9:14-50	Ps. 48:1-8
7-Mar	Num. 4	Mark 10:1-34	Ps. 48:9-14
8-Mar	Num. 5:1-6:21	Mark 10:35-52	Ps. 49:1-9
9-Mar	Num. 6:22-7:47	Mark 11	Ps. 49:10-20
10-Mar	Num. 7:48-8:4	Mark 12:1-27	Ps. 50:1-15
11-Mar	Num. 8:5-9:23	Mark 12:28-44	Ps. 50:16-23
12-Mar	Num. 10-11	Mark 13:1-8	Ps. 51:1-9
13-Mar	Num. 12-13	Mark 13:9-37	Ps. 51:10-19
14-Mar	Num. 14	Mark 14:1-31	Ps. 52
15-Mar	Num. 15	Mark 14:32-72	Ps. 53
16-Mar	Num. 16	Mark 15:1-32	Ps. 54
17-Mar	Num. 17-18	Mark 15:33-47	Ps. 55
18-Mar	Num. 19-20	Mark 16	Ps. 56:1-7
19-Mar	Num. 21:1-22:20	Luke 1:1-25	Ps. 56:8-13
20-Mar	Num. 22:21-23:30	Luke 1:26-56	Ps. 57
21-Mar	Num. 24-25	Luke 1:57-2:20	Ps. 58
22-Mar	Num. 26:1-27:11	Luke 2:21-38	Ps. 59:1-8
23-Mar	Num. 27:12-29:11	Luke 2:39-52	Ps. 59:9-17
24-Mar	Num. 29:12-30:16	Luke 3	Ps. 60:1-5
25-Mar	Num. 31	Luke 4	Ps. 60:6-12
26-Mar	Num. 32-33	Luke 5:1-16	Ps. 61
27-Mar	Num. 34-36	Luke 5:17-32	Ps. 62:1-6
28-Mar	Deut. 1:1-2:25	Luke 5:33-6:11	Ps. 62:7-12
29-Mar	Deut. 2:26-4:14	Luke 6:12-35	Ps. 63:1-5
30-Mar	Deut. 4:15-5:22	Luke 6:36-49	Ps. 63:6-11
31-Mar	Deut. 5:23-7:26	Luke 7:1-17	Ps. 64:1-5
1-Apr	Deut. 8-9	Luke 7:18-35	Ps. 64:6-10
2-Apr	Deut. 10-11	Luke 7:36-8:3	Ps. 65:1-8
3-Apr	Deut. 12-13	Luke 8:4-21	Ps. 65:9-13
4-Apr	Deut. 14:1-16:8	Luke 8:22-39	Ps. 66:1-7
5-Apr	Deut. 16:9-18:22	Luke 8:40-56	Ps. 66:8-15
6-Apr	Deut. 19:1-21:9	Luke 9:1-22	Ps. 66:16-20

7-Apr	Deut. 21:10-23:8	Luke 9:23-42	Ps. 67
8-Apr	Deut. 23:9-25:19	Luke 9:43-62	Ps. 68:1-6
9-Apr	Deut. 26:1-28:14	Luke 10:1-20	Ps. 68:7-14
10-Apr	Deut. 28:15-68	Luke 10:21-37	Ps. 68:15-19
11-Apr	Deut. 29-30	Luke 10:38-11:23	Ps. 68:20-27
12-Apr	Deut. 31:1-32:22	Luke 11:24-36	Ps. 68:28-35
13-Apr	Deut. 32:23-33:29	Luke 11:37-54	Ps. 69:1-9
14-Apr	Deut. 34-Josh. 2	Luke 12:1-15	Ps. 69:10-17
15-Apr	Josh. 3:1-5:12	Luke 12:16-40	Ps. 69:18-28
16-Apr	Josh. 5:13-7:26	Luke 12:41-48	Ps. 69:29-36
17-Apr	Josh. 8-9	Luke 12:49-59	Ps. 70
18-Apr	Josh. 10:1-11:15	Luke 13:1-21	Ps. 71:1-6
19-Apr	Josh. 11:16-13:33	Luke 13:22-35	Ps. 71:7-16
20-Apr	Josh. 14-16	Luke 14:1-15	Ps. 71:17-21
21-Apr	Josh. 17:1-19:16	Luke 14:16-35	Ps. 71:22-24
22-Apr	Josh. 19:17-21:42	Luke 15:1-10	Ps. 72:1-11
23-Apr	Josh. 21:43-22:34	Luke 15:11-32	Ps. 72:12-20
24-Apr	Josh. 23-24	Luke 16:1-18	Ps. 73:1-9
25-Apr	Judg. 1-2	Luke 16:19-17:10	Ps. 73:10-20
26-Apr	Judg. 3-4	Luke 17:11-37	Ps. 73:21-28
27-Apr	Judg. 5:1-6:24	Luke 18:1-17	Ps. 74:1-3
28-Apr	Judg. 6:25-7:25	Luke 18:18-43	Ps. 74:4-11
29-Apr	Judg. 8:1-9:23	Luke 19:1-28	Ps. 74:12-17
30-Apr	Judg. 9:24-10:18	Luke 19:29-48	Ps. 74:18-23
1-May	Judg. 11:1-12:7	Luke 20:1-26	Ps. 75:1-7
2-May	Judg. 12:8-14:20	Luke 20:27-47	Ps. 75:8-10
3-May	Judg. 15-16	Luke 21:1-19	Ps. 76:1-7
4-May	Judg. 17-18	Luke 21:20-22:6	Ps. 76:8-12
5-May	Judg. 19:1-20:23	Luke 22:7-30	Ps. 77:1-11
6-May	Judg. 20:24-21:25	Luke 22:31-54	Ps. 77:12-20
7-May	Ruth 1-2	Luke 22:55-23:25	Ps. 78:1-4
8-May	Ruth 3-4	Luke 23:26-24:12	Ps. 78:5-8

9-May	1 Sam. 1:1-2:21	Luke 24:13-53	Ps. 78:9-16
10-May	1 Sam. 2:22-4:22	John 1:1-28	Ps. 78:17-24
11-May	1 Sam. 5-7	John 1:29-51	Ps. 78:25-33
12-May	1 Sam. 8:1-9:26	John 2	Ps. 78:34-41
13-May	1 Sam. 9:27-11:15	John 3:1-22	Ps. 78:42-55
14-May	1 Sam. 12-13	John 3:23-4:10	Ps. 78:56-66
15-May	1 Sam. 14	John 4:11-38	Ps. 78:67-72
16-May	1 Sam. 15-16	John 4:39-54	Ps. 79:1-7
17-May	1 Sam. 17	John 5:1-24	Ps. 79:8-13
18-May	1 Sam. 18-19	John 5:25-47	Ps. 80:1-7
19-May	1 Sam. 20-21	John 6:1-21	Ps. 80:8-19
20-May	1 Sam. 22-23	John 6:22-42	Ps. 81:1-10
21-May	1 Sam. 24:1-25:31	John 6:43-71	Ps. 81:11-16
22-May	1 Sam. 25:32-27:12	John 7:1-24	Ps. 82
23-May	1 Sam. 28-29	John 7:25-8:11	Ps. 83
24-May	1 Sam. 30-31	John 8:12-47	Ps. 84:1-4
25-May	2 Sam. 1-2	John 8:48-9:12	Ps. 84:5-12
26-May	2 Sam. 3-4	John 9:13-34	Ps. 85:1-7
27-May	2 Sam. 5:1-7:17	John 9:35-10:10	Ps. 85:8-13
28-May	2 Sam. 7:18-10:19	John 10:11-30	Ps. 86:1-10
29-May	2 Sam. 11:1-12:25	John 10:31-11:16	Ps. 86:11-17
30-May	2 Sam. 12:26-13:39	John 11:17-54	Ps. 87
31-May	2 Sam. 14:1-15:12	John 11:55-12:19	Ps. 88:1-9
1-Jun	2 Sam. 15:13-16:23	John 12:20-43	Ps. 88:10-18
2-Jun	2 Sam. 17:1-18:18	John 12:44-13:20	Ps. 89:1-6
3-Jun	2 Sam. 18:19-19:39	John 13:21-38	Ps. 89:7-13
4-Jun	2 Sam. 19:40-21:22	John 14:1-17	Ps. 89:14-18
5-Jun	2 Sam. 22:1-23:7	John 14:18-15:27	Ps. 89:19-29
6-Jun	2 Sam. 23:8-24:25	John 16:1-22	Ps. 89:30-37
7-Jun	1 Kings 1	John 16:23-17:5	Ps. 89:38-52
8-Jun	1 Kings 2	John 17:6-26	Ps. 90:1-12
9-Jun	1 Kings 3-4	John 18:1-27	Ps. 90:13-17

10-Jun	1 Kings 5-6	John 18:28-19:5	Ps. 91:1-10
11-Jun	1 Kings 7	John 19:6-25a	Ps. 91:11-16
12-Jun	1 Kings 8:1-53	John 19:25b-42	Ps. 92:1-9
13-Jun	1 Kings 8:54-10:13	John 20:1-18	Ps. 92:10-15
14-Jun	1 Kings 10:14-11:43	John 20:19-31	Ps. 93
15-Jun	1 Kings 12:1-13:10	John 21	Ps. 94:1-11
16-Jun	1 Kings 13:11-14:31	Acts 1:1-11	Ps. 94:12-23
17-Jun	1 Kings 15:1-16:20	Acts 1:12-26	Ps. 95
18-Jun	1 Kings 16:21-18:19	Acts 2:1-21	Ps. 96:1-8
19-Jun	1 Kings 18:20-19:21	Acts2:22-41	Ps. 96:9-13
20-Jun	1 Kings 20	Acts 2:42-3:26	Ps. 97:1-6
21-Jun	1 Kings 21:1-22:28	Acts 4:1-22	Ps. 97:7-12
22-Jun	1 Kings 22:29- 2 Kings 1:18	Acts 4:23-5:11	Ps. 98
23-Jun	2 Kings 2-3	Acts 5:12-28	Ps. 99
24-Jun	2 Kings 4	Acts 5:29-6:15	Ps. 100
25-Jun	2 Kings 5:1-6:23	Acts 7:1-16	Ps. 101
26-Jun	2 Kings 6:24-8:15	Acts 7:17-36	Ps. 102:1-7
27-Jun	2 Kings 8:16-9:37	Acts 7:37-53	Ps. 102:8-17
28-Jun	2 Kings 10-11	Acts 7:54-8:8	Ps. 102:18-28
29-Jun	2 Kings 12-13	Acts 8:9-40	Ps. 103:1-9
30-Jun	2 Kings 14-15	Acts 9:1-16	Ps. 103:10-14
1-Jul	2 Kings 16-17	Acts 9:17-31	Ps. 103:15-22
2-Jul	2 Kings 18:1-19:7	Acts 9:32-10:16	Ps. 104:1-9
3-Jul	2 Kings 19:8-20:21	Acts 10:17-33	Ps. 104:10-23
4-Jul	2 Kings 21:1-22:20	Acts 10:34-11:18	Ps. 104: 24-30
5-Jul	2 Kings 23	Acts 11:19-12:17	Ps. 104:31-35
6-Jul	2 Kings 24-25	Acts 12:18-13:13	Ps. 105:1-7
7-Jul	1 Chron. 1-2	Acts 13:14-43	Ps. 105:8-15
8-Jul	1 Chron. 3:1-5:10	Acts 13:44-14:10	Ps. 105:16-28
9-Jul	1 Chron. 5:11-6:81	Acts 14:11-28	Ps. 105:29-36
10-Jul	1 Chron. 7:1-9:9	Acts 15:1-18	Ps. 105:37-45

11-Jul	1 Chron. 9:10-11:9	Acts 15:19-41	Ps. 106:1-12
12-Jul	1 Chron. 11:10-12:40	Acts 16:1-15	Ps. 106:13-27
13-Jul	1 Chron. 13-15	Acts 16:16-40	Ps. 106:28-33
14-Jul	1 Chron. 16-17	Acts 17:1-14	Ps. 106:34-43
15-Jul	1 Chron. 18-20	Acts 17:15-34	Ps. 106:44-48
16-Jul	1 Chron. 21-22	Acts 18:1-23	Ps. 107:1-9
17-Jul	1 Chron. 23-25	Acts 18:24-19:10	Ps. 107:10-16
18-Jul	1 Chron. 26-27	Acts 19:11-22	Ps. 107:17-32
19-Jul	1 Chron. 28-29	Acts 19:23-41	Ps. 107:33-38
20-Jul	2 Chron. 1-3	Acts 20:1-16	Ps. 107:39-43
21-Jul	2 Chron. 4:1-6:11	Acts 20:17-38	Ps. 108
22-Jul	2 Chron. 6:12-7:10	Acts 21:1-14	Ps. 109:1-20
23-Jul	2 Chron. 7:11-9:28	Acts 21:15-32	Ps. 109:21-31
24-Jul	2 Chron. 9:29-12:16	Acts 21:33-22:16	Ps. 110:1-3
25-Jul	2 Chron. 13-15	Acts 22:17-23:11	Ps. 110:4-7
26-Jul	2 Chron. 16-17	Acts 23:12-24:21	Ps. 111
27-Jul	2 Chron. 18-19	Acts 24:22-25:12	Ps. 112
28-Jul	2 Chron. 20-21	Acts 25:13-27	Ps. 113
29-Jul	2 Chron. 22-23	Acts 26	Ps. 114
30-Jul	2 Chron. 24:1-25:16	Acts 27:1-20	Ps. 115:1-10
31-Jul	2 Chron. 25:17-27:9	Acts 27:21-28:6	Ps. 115:11-18
1-Aug	2 Chron. 28:1-29:19	Acts 28:7-31	Ps. 116:1-5
2-Aug	2 Chron. 29:20-30:27	Rom. 1:1-17	Ps. 116:6-19
3-Aug	2 Chron. 31-32	Rom. 1:18-32	Ps. 117
4-Aug	2 Chron. 33:1-34:7	Rom. 2	Ps. 118:1-18
5-Aug	2 Chron. 34:8-35:19	Rom. 3:1-26	Ps. 118:19-23
6-Aug	2 Chron. 35:20-36:23	Rom. 3:27-4:25	Ps. 118:24-29
7-Aug	Ezra 1-3	Rom. 5	Ps. 119:1-8
8-Aug	Ezra 4-5	Rom. 6:1-7:6	Ps. 119:9-16
9-Aug	Ezra 6:1-7:26	Rom. 7:7-25	Ps. 119:17-32
10-Aug	Ezra 7:27-9:4	Rom. 8:1-27	Ps. 119:33-40
11-Aug	Ezra 9:5-10:44	Rom. 8:28-39	Ps. 119:41-64

12-Aug	Neh. 1:1-3:16	Rom. 9:1-18	Ps. 119:65-72
13-Aug	Neh. 3:17-5:13	Rom. 9:19-33	Ps. 119:73-80
14-Aug	Neh. 5:14-7:73	Rom. 10:1-13	Ps. 119:81-88
15-Aug	Neh. 8:1-9:5	Rom. 10:14-11:24	Ps. 119:89-104
16-Aug	Neh. 9:6-10:27	Rom. 11:25-12:8	Ps. 119:105-120
17-Aug	Neh. 10:28-12:26	Rom. 12:9-13:7	Ps. 119:121-128
18-Aug	Neh. 12:27-13:31	Rom. 13:8-14:12	Ps. 119:129-136
19-Aug	Esther 1:1-2:18	Rom. 14:13-15:13	Ps. 119:137-152
20-Aug	Esther 2:19-5:14	Rom. 15:14-21	Ps. 119:153-168
21-Aug	Esther. 6-8	Rom. 15:22-33	Ps. 119:169-176
22-Aug	Esther 9-10	Rom. 16	Ps. 120-122
23-Aug	Job 1-3	1 Cor. 1:1-25	Ps. 123
24-Aug	Job 4-6	1 Cor. 1:26-2:16	Ps. 124-125
25-Aug	Job 7-9	1 Cor. 3	Ps. 126-127
26-Aug	Job 10-13	1 Cor. 4:1-13	Ps. 128-129
27-Aug	Job 14-16	1 Cor. 4:14-5:13	Ps. 130
28-Aug	Job 17-20	1 Cor. 6	Ps. 131
29-Aug	Job 21-23	1 Cor. 7:1-16	Ps. 132
30-Aug	Job 24-27	1 Cor. 7:17-40	Ps. 133-134
31-Aug	Job 28-30	1 Cor. 8	Ps. 135
1-Sep	Job 31-33	1 Cor. 9:1-18	Ps. 136:1-9
2-Sep	Job 34-36	1 Cor. 9:19-10:13	Ps. 136:10-26
3-Sep	Job 37-39	1 Cor. 10:14-11:1	Ps. 137
4-Sep	Job 40-42	1 Cor. 11:2-34	Ps. 138
5-Sep	Eccles. 1:1-3:15	1 Cor. 12:1-26	Ps. 139:1-6
6-Sep	Eccles. 3:16-6:12	1 Cor. 12:27-13:13	Ps. 139:7-18
7-Sep	Eccles. 7:1-9:12	1 Cor. 14:1-22	Ps. 139:19-24
8-Sep	Eccles. 9:13-12:14	1 Cor. 14:23-15:11	Ps. 140:1-8
9-Sep	SS 1-4	1 Cor. 15:12-34	Ps. 140:9-13
10-Sep	SS 5-8	1 Cor. 15:35-58	Ps. 141
11-Sep	Isa. 1-2	1 Cor. 16	Ps. 142
12-Sep	Isa. 3-5	2 Cor. 1:1-11	Ps. 143:1-6

13-Sep	Isa. 6-8	2 Cor. 1:12-2:4	Ps. 143:7-12
14-Sep	Isa. 9-10	2 Cor. 2:5-17	Ps. 144
15-Sep	Isa. 11-13	2 Cor. 3	Ps. 145
16-Sep	Isa. 14-16	2 Cor. 4	Ps. 146
17-Sep	Isa. 17-19	2 Cor. 5	Ps. 147:1-11
18-Sep	Isa. 20-23	2 Cor. 6	Ps. 147:12-20
19-Sep	Isa. 24:1-26:19	2 Cor. 7	Ps. 148
20-Sep	Isa. 26:20-28:29	2 Cor. 8	Ps. 149-150
21-Sep	Isa. 29-30	2 Cor. 9	Prov. 1:1-9
22-Sep	Isa. 31-33	2 Cor. 10	Prov. 1:10-22
23-Sep	Isa. 34-36	2 Cor. 11	Prov. 1:23-26
24-Sep	Isa. 37-38	2 Cor. 12:1-10	Prov. 1:27-33
25-Sep	Isa. 39-40	2 Cor. 12:11-13:14	Prov. 2:1-15
26-Sep	Isa. 41-42	Gal. 1	Prov. 2:16-22
27-Sep	Isa. 43:1-44:20	Gal. 2	Prov. 3:1-12
28-Sep	Isa. 44:21-46:13	Gal. 3:1-18	Prov. 3:13-26
29-Sep	Isa. 47:1-49:13	Gal 3:19-29	Prov. 3:27-35
30-Sep	Isa. 49:14-51:23	Gal 4:1-11	Prov. 4:1-19
1-Oct	Isa. 52-54	Gal. 4:12-31	Prov. 4:20-27
2-Oct	Isa. 55-57	Gal. 5	Prov. 5:1-14
3-Oct	Isa. 58-59	Gal. 6	Prov. 5:15-23
4-Oct	Isa. 60-62	Eph. 1	Prov. 6:1-5
5-Oct	Isa. 63:1-65:16	Eph. 2	Prov. 6:6-19
6-Oct	Isa. 65:17-66:24	Eph. 3:1-4:16	Prov. 6:20-26
7-Oct	Jer. 1-2	Eph. 4:17-32	Prov. 6:27-35
8-Oct	Jer. 3:1-4:22	Eph. 5	Prov. 7:1-5
9-Oct	Jer. 4:23-5:31	Eph. 6	Prov. 7:6-27
10-Oct	Jer. 6:1-7:26	Phil. 1:1-26	Prov. 8:1-11
11-Oct	Jer. 7:26-9:16	Phil. 1:27-2:18	Prov. 8:12-21
12-Oct	Jer. 9:17-11:17	Phil 2:19-30	Prov. 8:22-36
13-Oct	Jer. 11:18-13:27	Phil. 3	Prov. 9:1-6
14-Oct	Jer. 14-15	Phil. 4	Prov. 9:7-18

16-Nov	Ezek. 20	Heb. 10:1-25	Prov. 18:18-24
17-Nov	Ezek. 21-22	Heb. 10:26-39	Prov. 19:1-8
18-Nov	Ezek. 23	Heb. 11:1-31	Prov. 19:9-14
19-Nov	Ezek. 24-26	Heb. 11:32-40	Prov. 19:15-21
20-Nov	Ezek. 27-28	Heb. 12:1-13	Prov. 19:22-29
21-Nov	Ezek. 29-30	Heb. 12:14-29	Prov. 20:1-18
22-Nov	Ezek. 31-32	Heb. 13	Prov. 20:19-24
23-Nov	Ezek. 33:1-34:10	Jas. 1	Prov. 20:25-30
24-Nov	Ezek. 34:11-36:15	Jas. 2	Prov. 21:1-8
25-Nov	Ezek. 36:16-37:28	Jas. 3	Prov. 21:9-18
26-Nov	Ezek. 38-39	Jas. 4:1-5:6	Prov. 21:19-24
27-Nov	Ezek. 40	Jas. 5:7-20	Prov. 21:25-31
28-Nov	Ezek. 41:1-43:12	1 Pet. 1:1-12	Prov. 22:1-9
29-Nov	Ezek. 43:13-44:31	1 Pet. 1:13-2:3	Prov. 22:10-23
30-Nov	Ezek. 45-46	1 Pet. 2:4-17	Prov. 22:24-29
1-Dec	Ezek. 47-48	1 Pet. 2:18-3:7	Prov. 23:1-9
2-Dec	Dan. 1:1-2:23	1 Pet. 3:8-4:19	Prov. 23:10-16
3-Dec	Dan. 2:24-3:30	1 Pet. 5	Prov. 23:17-25
4-Dec	Dan. 4	2 Pet. 1	Prov. 23:26-35
5-Dec	Dan. 5	2 Pet. 2	Prov. 24:1-18
6-Dec	Dan. 6:1-7:14	2 Pet. 3	Prov. 24:19-27
7-Dec	Dan. 7:15-8:27	1 John 1:1-2:17	Prov. 24:28-34
8-Dec	Dan. 9-10	1 John 2:18-29	Prov. 25:1-12
9-Dec	Dan. 11-12	1 John 3:1-12	Prov. 25:13-17
10-Dec	Hos. 1-3	1 John 3:13-4:16	Prov. 25:18-28
11-Dec	Hos. 4-6	1 John 4:17-5:21	Prov. 26:1-16
12-Dec	Hos. 7-10	2 John	Prov. 26:17-21
13-Dec	Hos. 11-14	3 John	Prov. 26:22-27:9
14-Dec	Joel 1:1-2:17	Jude	Prov. 27:10-17
15-Dec	Joel 2:18-3:21	Rev. 1:1-2:11	Prov. 27:18-27
16-Dec	Amos 1:1-4:5	Rev. 2:12-29	Prov. 28:1-8
17-Dec	Amos 4:6-6:14	Rev. 3	Prov. 28:9-16

*Enjoy the
following pages from*

*Secrets of the
Proverbs 31 Woman*

by Rae Simons

Introduction

The book of Proverbs is full of word pictures that help us understand deep truths. One that recurs again and again is the comparison of wisdom to a woman. This woman is strong and outspoken; she shouts in the streets (1:20). In the long passage found in the thirty-first chapter we learn still more about her.

Verse after verse, this passage of scripture affirms our identity as women. The woman we see in Proverbs 31 is committed to her relationships; her husband and children depend on her and are blessed by her. She works hard and efficiently, with initiative and creativity. She knows how to use her skills to make money, but she also reaches out to those in need. She takes care of herself as well.

Each detail is not meant to describe a specific, single woman. In other words, we don't need to add them to our to-do lists! Instead, Proverbs 31 shows us a larger picture of what we are all capable of being as women. It's like a mirror God holds up for us to look into—and then He says, "See? This is who I created you to be."

As women, God calls us to embody love and wisdom. Each of us will do that differently, with our unique skills and individual strengths—but we all have amazing things to offer the world. We don't need to be afraid to be strong, to be wise, to try new things. God believes in us!

This is the sort of book that's intended to be read slowly, one meditation at a time. Doing so will give you time to ponder each section of this scripture and apply it to your own life. Hear what God has to say to you through the Proverbs 31 woman!

Part I

Who can find a virtuous woman?
for her price is far above rubies.

—verse 10 KJV

Strong, Capable, Creative

When you hear the phrase *virtuous woman*, what does it call to mind? Most of us probably think of a "good woman," someone who obeys the Bible and avoids sin. Personally, I picture a matronly woman dressed in a modest, nondescript dress, with a calm look on her face. Sadly, I don't identify with this woman because I know I fall far short of her serenity and purity. And if I'm honest—well, frankly, I find her a little boring.

As twenty-first-century women, we find it hard to reconcile our own lives with the ancient standard of excellence offered to us in Proverbs. Our culture today is so different from that which existed in the Near East, hundreds of years before Christ. Adding to our difficulty, Christian men through the centuries have held up these verses to their wives and daughters as the perfect example of what a Christian woman should be. Sometimes, as women, we may feel a little resentful at having so much "goodness" demanded of us!

Our discomfort with these verses may be caused in part, though, simply because of differences in our twenty-first-century language from that used when the King James Bible was written. If you look up the word *virtuous* in a modern dictionary, you'll find that it means "righteous, morally upright, saintly, principled, ethical." There's nothing wrong with being all those things, of course! But this definition isn't quite what the ancient author had in mind, and it wasn't what the seventeenth-century translators were shooting for either when they used the word *virtuous*. Back in the 1600s, someone who was virtuous was strong and courageous, filled with power to bring about good in the world. It was a word used to describe knights, not meek little women!

If we turn to other versions of the Bible, we find that where the King James Version uses *virtuous*, more modern translations of Proverbs offer words like *excellent*, *capable*, *diligent*, *noble*, and *worthy*. These words get us a little closer to what the ancient author had in mind millennia ago when he composed these verses.

The Hebrew word used here points us even more directly back to the seventeenth-century understanding of what it meant to be virtuous. The word is *chayil*, and according to Strong's Concordance, it means "strong, effective, and brave." It's a word that was used to describe armies, troops that were valiant and mighty, with plenty of resources to draw from.

Our modern-day society often considers goodness to be boring, but earlier cultures knew it was just the opposite. Good people are strong and brave; they're the people who change the world for the better; they're the people God uses to accomplish amazing things. When the ancient author of Proverbs wrote this passage, he wasn't imagining a woman who was the least bit dull!

In fact, the Bible's image of the perfect woman was pretty radical. During pre-Christian Bible times, women were generally considered to be second-rate people, inferior to men—but these verses in Proverbs offered a far different perspective. The Proverbs 31 woman was strong, capable, and creative.

These words, written thousands of years ago, still inspire and challenge us as women today. God is calling us to be like valiant knights in shining armor, riding out to bring God's justice and love to the world around us.

Dear God, I ask that You help me be truly virtuous.
Make me strong with Your strength and courageous
with Your courage. Use me to do great things.

How Will We Live?

The word *virtue* shows up throughout the Bible. When we look at how it's used in other scripture verses, we may get an even better idea of what it means to be a "virtuous woman."

In 2 Peter 1:5, Peter writes, "Giving all diligence, add to your faith virtue; and to virtue knowledge" (KJV). He's telling us that we need to support our trust in God with virtue's active goodness. In other words, our faith inspires us to take action! It gives us energy to accomplish great things, but we don't just run around doing everything we can think of; we temper our virtue with understanding and wisdom.

When the psalmist wrote, "They go from strength to strength, till each appears before God in Zion" (Psalm 84:7 NIV), the Hebrew word translated as "strength" is the same as that translated as "virtuous" in Proverbs 31, and once again, it's connected to well-supplied armies that can fight confidently and bravely. The promise here is given to all of us who "dwell in God's house": we will increase in power, in courage, and in our ability to do God's work.

In the book of Ruth, when Boaz announced to his community that he was going to marry Ruth, the elders said to him, "May the LORD make the woman who is coming into your home like Rachel and Leah, both of whom built the house of Israel; and may you achieve wealth in Ephrathah" (4:11 NASB). In this verse, the Hebrew word translated "wealth" is *chayil*, the same word used for "virtue" in Proverbs 31. The Jewish elders were comparing Ruth, a woman from Moab, to Rachel and Leah, two of the great women of the Old Testament whose energy and courage helped make Israel a strong nation.

So what does that mean to us today as women? If we are virtuous women, how will we live? How will we think of ourselves?

Lord of my life, I ask that You help me see myself with Your eyes. May I see the strong woman You have called to serve You. Wipe away my self-doubt. Heal my sense that I'm not good enough, talented enough, smart enough, or capable enough. I believe in You, Lord, and I ask You now to add energy and courage to my belief.

I put myself in Your hands, trusting that You will lead me from strength to strength. Make me like Ruth, like Rachel and Leah. Use me to build Your house.

Women Of Virtue

When the ancient author sat down to write these verses in Proverbs, I wonder if he had a real woman in mind, someone he knew. Was it his own wife who inspired him to write these words? Or his mother? Did he realize that the world is full of women of strength and courage, women with an active faith in God who work hard to make the world a better place for all of us?

When I look at my own experience, I see how women of virtue have shaped my life. I think of my mother reading to me every night before I went to bed, even when she was falling asleep herself after a long day of work. I think of my mother-in-law who always welcomed us to a house that was filled with the scent of fresh-made tomato sauce. I think of my grandmothers, each with her own brand of resolute courage in the face of hardship. I think of my friends and sisters, women who have known me all my life, who love me and forgive me and understand me, year after year. I think of my teachers and mentors, women who showed me how to grow, how to go further and climb higher, both professionally and spiritually.

We all have women like these in our lives. And when we look at history, we see other women of virtue, a long chain of women that spans the centuries. The great women of the Old Testament—Sarah, Esther, and Deborah, for example—give us examples of women who were neither meek nor boring; instead, they were strong-minded, active women who stood up courageously for their people. If we shift our attention to more recent history, women like Harriet Beecher Stowe and Florence Nightingale once again proved that courageous women could change the world for the better. Harriet Beecher Stowe's book, *Uncle Tom's Cabin*, so powerfully influenced readers' minds that it helped to bring about the end of slavery in the United States, while Florence Nightingale improved soldiers' wartime medical treatment as she also opened up the field of nursing to women. In the twentieth century, Rosa Parks's courage sparked the civil rights movement, and Mother Teresa's devotion to the poor inspired the world to do more for those in need. All of these women lived lives of faith and commitment, giving all of their strength to serve God and others.

Today, we can be both challenged and encouraged by the women of virtue who have gone before us. From our perspective, these women may seem like extraordinary heroines—but from their own, they were just ordinary women who got up each morning and did ordinary things with love and commitment. Doing those "ordinary things" over and over and over sometimes takes the most courage and strength of all—and those seemingly small things are often what God uses to change the world.

> *Dear God, I thank You for the women of virtue who*
> *have gone before me. Thank You for all the ways You*
> *used them to bring Your love to me and to the world.*
> *May I be inspired by their examples. Use me, I pray,*
> *as You used them. May I too work courageously for*
> *Your kingdom. I give myself to You, Lord.*

Treasures Within

According to the author of Proverbs, the price of a virtuous woman "is far above rubies" (KJV). At first glance, I'm not sure I like the idea that a woman has a price, even if it's a high one. Women aren't chattel, after all; we can't be bought and sold. But when I look again, I realize that is exactly what the scripture is saying: no price whatsoever can be put on the virtuous woman because she is not something that can be purchased. In fact, she is more valuable than any material wealth.

Besides a virtuous woman, there's only one other thing in the Bible that's said to be more valuable than rubies—wisdom. Proverbs 3:15 tells us that wisdom is "more precious than rubies; nothing you desire can compare with her" (NIV). Job 28:18 says that "the price of wisdom is above rubies" (KJV), and we read in Proverbs 20:15 that "wise words are more valuable than. . .rubies" (NLT). By implication then, Proverbs 31 is comparing a virtuous woman to wisdom. That's quite a compliment!

Wisdom is more than intelligence, and it's far deeper than mere knowledge. Wisdom is one of God's own attributes. According to the Bible, the wise person doesn't just follow all the rules but instead acts, thinks, and lives in total harmony with God's will.

Wisdom is another aspect of a Proverbs 31 woman's virtue. A woman of virtue lives in harmony with God, and that harmony spreads out through her life. As a result, she also lives in harmony with other people. Wisdom leads her to act in ways that bring peace between herself and those around her, and wisdom also brings her into harmony with herself. As she allows herself to be caught up in God's will, she finds a sense of self-worth and inner peace. She knows her value comes from God.

Aristotle said, "Knowing yourself is the beginning of wisdom." When we start to get to know ourselves, we will also get to know God—and when we get to know God, we will also understand our own selves better. It works both ways.

This is the source of our wisdom as women: we are on a journey of discovery with God. He is pointing out in us the things He values; He is revealing places where we can grow; and He is leading us into an adventure that will last our entire lifetimes—and continue on even after this life. Who knows what treasures we will discover within God and within our own hearts along the way?

*Dear Lord, thank You that You treasure me.
Help me know my true worth in Your eyes. Teach
me to follow wisdom. As I journey through life,
help me live in complete harmony with You.*

More Valuable Than Rubies

As women, many of us struggle with our self-concepts. We live in a world that tells us we have to measure up to multiple standards. We have to prove our worth again and again, in all sorts of ways.

First of all, we have to look a certain way. We need to have bodies that are shaped according to the standards our society considers beautiful (no matter how impossible they may be for most women to attain). Our hair needs to be in style, our clothes fashionable, and our faces perfectly made up. When we step on the scales, we need to see numbers that are closer to one hundred than two hundred!

At the same time, we need to juggle all the roles we fill. Many of us are working women who need to compete in the professional world. We have to be on time, be efficient, keep our cool, pay attention, work to get to the top, and earn enough to help support our families. At the same time, though, we need to be able to care for our families. We nurture children and older parents. We are faithful and sensitive friends, and we are loving wives. But that's not all! We also have to keep our houses clean. . .prepare meals. . .volunteer at church and in our communities. . .and somehow stay calm through it all. Most of all, we want to make everyone happy. We want to do everything we can to make everyone like us!

When we can't achieve all this—and who can?—our sense of our own value plummets. We compare ourselves to those around us, who all seem to be doing so much better than we are at being pretty, smart, accomplished, loving, and loved women. We become discouraged and full of despair. We doubt our own worth.

But Proverbs 31 doesn't say that our value is based on any of these things. Instead, it says that when we are women of virtue—women of strength and courage—then we are worth more than any jewel. It doesn't say anything at all about our worth depending on how clean our houses are or how much we weigh. Or even on how much other people like us!

God doesn't care about any of the standards we so often use to define ourselves. Whether we are overweight or slender, well dressed or scarecrows, slobs or tidy, professionals or stay-at-home moms, popular or social misfits, we are all equally treasured. We are more valuable than rubies because God has filled us with virtue!

Loving God, You know how hard I try to be everything that's expected of me. I wear myself out working so hard to be good at all the roles I fill. I truly want to be good at each of the jobs I do, both at home and at work. And I want so much to make those I love happy. When I start to focus too much on these things, though, I ask that You remind me to shift my attention to You. Help me rely on Your perspective instead of society's. Give me confidence in the strength You have given me—strength to love, strength to serve You, strength to do good in the world.

Part II

*Her husband has full confidence
in her and lacks nothing of value.
She brings him good, not harm,
all the days of her life.*

—verses 11–12 NIV

Deep Enough

The husband of the Proverbs 31 woman trusts her completely because she's proven herself trustworthy. At first it's tempting to skip over that statement quickly, thinking to ourselves, *Of course I'm trustworthy. I'd never cheat on my husband. And I do more than my part to make this marriage work. My husband isn't lacking anything, not on my account!* But sometimes we should take another honest look at ourselves. Can our husbands trust us to understand them, even when understanding might ask us to adjust our own thinking or behaviors? Do they lack our respect when it comes to their interests and emotions? Do we ever hurt their feelings? Are we impatient with them, easily irritated? Is it truly our goal to bring our husbands "good, not harm" each and every day?

Many times, I suspect, we're so busy with our many responsibilities that our husbands' needs fall into the background. Instead, we're likely to be far more aware of all the ways we wish they would help us out—and then we feel frustrated and angry if they don't. Our own needs are at the forefront of our consciousness. When we think of our husbands, we often tend to focus on what we get from them emotionally—and we may complain a lot about what we don't get! We may be far less aware of our own shortcomings in the relationship.

This doesn't mean we need to be doormat wives, submissive in the old-fashioned sense of the word. God doesn't ask us to be untrue to our own needs or to deny our God-given identities. We might want to ask ourselves these questions instead: "Is my husband as real to me as I am to myself? Or do I see him as someone

I expect to be there at my convenience, someone whose job is to make my life easier? Do I see his needs as being as important as my own? Do I accept him unconditionally?"

Psychologist Carl Rogers referred to "unconditional positive regard" when he wrote about the important components of a healthy relationship. The ability to care about your partner—and communicate your concern without a lot of judgmental stuff thrown in—is the essence of a healthy intimate relationship.

It's not easy, of course. But no one ever said marriage was easy! Being married isn't a decision you can make once and then be done with it. The wedding ceremony does not magically transform us into "married people." Instead, being married is a lifetime process, one we must commit ourselves to again and again. We must choose to be married daily—and that means choosing to go past our own immature, selfish emotions. It means choosing to go deep enough that our husbands can trust us to bring them only good.

God of love, thank You for my husband. Give me strength today to look past my preoccupation with myself. Help me truly see this man I'm married to. Show me where I have failed to understand him, where I have been too preoccupied with my own concerns to see his. Let me find ways to bring good into his life.

Leap Of Faith

"You're acting like a selfish princess," we used to say to our daughter when she was younger. But I have to admit I have a selfish princess who lives inside me as well. She's the one who always wants to be in control. She wants her husband to make her life easier, not harder. Actually, she kind of treats him like her slave.

And when he doesn't always cooperate, I'm as frustrated and angry as any four-year-old. When my requests turn into demands, however, I'm failing to respect my husband's personhood. He is not my slave; he was not put on earth for my sole convenience. Slavery sees another human being as a mere object, but true love honors that person.

Married partners are called "helpmeets" because they are in fact intended to help each other. I often expect my husband's help—for everything from killing spiders to opening cans—and I admit he seldom asks me for anything in return that I find unreasonable or too demanding. Sometimes he asks me to scratch his back or get him a drink when he's working. Most of the time he doesn't exactly ask, he just hints—like when I haven't made his favorite meal in a while. By the same token, sometimes when we're both in bed, I'll start complaining about how thirsty I am; he'll groan, but he gets up to get me a glass of water.

But those are simple requests. It's easy to look only at them and give myself a pat on the back for being such a good wife. But then another recent event comes to mind.

Our family car needed repairs, and my husband and I had agreed to meet at a certain time at the service station. We would leave the family car, and then I'd take the car he usually drives and drop him off back at work. I then needed to be at an appointment, and I had several other responsibilities I had to fit in before the end of the workday. The schedule I had planned for myself was a tight one, so I was irritated when I arrived at the service station and found that my husband wasn't there. When I called him, he asked me in a brusque voice to wait for him a bit longer.

An hour ticked away. I had to call and cancel my appointment. I kept looking at the time and feeling more and more frustrated. There was no way now I could get everything done that I had to do. I felt totally out of control of my own life, and I resented my husband for doing that to me. By the time he arrived, I was furious.

"How can you be so selfish?" I demanded. "Does it ever occur to you that I have things to do too?" I may have said a few other things as well.

He gave me a quick, angry answer. His voice was defensive, and he barely looked at me. In fact, he seemed preoccupied, as though he could not have cared less about my disrupted day. *What a jerk,* I thought to myself as I dropped him off at work. We didn't even say goodbye as he got out and hurried back into his workplace.

By the time he came home that night, I was sorry for losing my temper. I was even sorrier when I learned he had been in the middle of a safety crisis at work, something he couldn't discuss until it was over. But I didn't trust him enough to give him the help he needed without complaint. I wasn't thinking about doing good for him. (Mostly, I was just thinking about how much I wanted to clobber him.)

It doesn't come naturally to lay aside our own personal agendas —especially if we don't see a good reason why we should. Sometimes it means taking a small leap of sheer, blind faith. When we do, we give our husbands reason to have confidence in us.

Dear Jesus, when You were on earth, You were always true to Yourself—and yet at the same time, You gave Yourself in love to others. Show me how to do the same with my husband. May I not be so quick to get angry. Instead, teach me to rely more on Your love, knowing that You will work out everything—even my tight schedule—to the glory of God.

Let Love Flow

How often do you tell your husband you love him? It's a simple habit to form—and the more often we say the words, the more secure our husbands will feel. It's a habit that pays off in other ways as well.

Sometimes we get in vicious circles where we snap at our husbands. . .they feel hurt and exasperated, so they give an angry retort. . .we're hurt by their angry voices, so we go on the defensive. . .and the circle goes around and around until something or someone breaks it. But we can choose to form "loving circles" instead. Psychologists have found that the more often we express love, the more loving we tend to feel. This productive and kind cycle strengthens the feeling that inspires the words, and on and on.

We don't have to wait for our husbands to be the first to start these loving cycles. The more we express our love to our husbands, the more likely they are to respond with their own expressions of love, forming another beneficial and creative circle to replace the vicious circles we all fall into so easily.

Marriage is an opportunity to let God's love flow through us. Our culture usually looks at things differently; most people spend their lives looking for ways that others can be of use to them. We may have entered marriage with that same attitude, expecting our husbands to make us feel loved, rather than seeking opportunities to demonstrate our love to them. Often, we wait to be told we're loved before we'll respond in kind. Even within the marriage commitment, we want to know we're secure before we'll lay our hearts out where they might be hurt.

But that's not the way God loves. God's love is completely vulnerable. There are no self-protective barriers around it. It gives without thought of return. It doesn't wait for us to love God back. It simply pours into our lives, no matter how often we reject it and turn away from it, no matter how many times we're too focused on our concerns to even notice it.

What would happen if we tried to love our husbands that way?

Dear God, each of my days is filled with Your love. Everywhere I turn, I see Your love—in the world of nature, in my friends, in my family, in Your Spirit filling my heart. You never hold back Your love. You give it freely, unconditionally, endlessly. I know I can never hope to love as perfectly as You do, but may I seek to model my love for my husband after Your love. May I be quick to express love, slow to express anger and impatience. May I be thoughtful of his needs, as sensitive to his feelings as I am to my own. Help me be a channel through which Your love can flow to my husband.

Warm, Sweet Junes

Our romantic fairy-tale view of marriage leads us to expect that once two people marry, they will be happy forevermore, end of story. So when we run into long stretches of boredom or unhappiness, we doubt our love. After all, according to the dictates of our culture, if we're not happy, then something is wrong—and we often assume the fault lies with our husbands. Clearly, they don't love us enough! If they did, we'd be happy. We'd still feel that same love and joy we felt at the beginning of our relationships. That sense of "something wrong" can make us build walls around our hearts. We feel as though we need to withdraw from our husbands, put up our defenses. It seems perfectly sensible to place our own needs first. We lose confidence in our husbands—and in return, we give them reason to lose confidence in us.

These times come to even the strongest marriages, particularly during the early years, before experience gives us greater perspective. As the years go by, though, we may learn that, like the seasons, married love has cycles. Sometimes our marriages may seem as cold and dead as January—but if we wait, if we're patient, spring always comes once more. Then we may find ourselves surprised—and delighted—to be falling in love with our husbands all over again. It would be easier to run away the first time November's chilly gray skies settle over our marriages. But just think of all the warm, sweet Junes we would miss if we did!

Romantic books and movies don't prepare us for marriage's reality. From the time we were children, we were raised on the words, "And they lived happily ever after." No one ever mentioned that happiness is hard work. But the truth is, after we've fallen into each other's arms and declared our mutual passion, after we've gone still further and said, "I do," that's when the real story begins. And that story is full of joy and tenderness—but it's also full of frustration and self-discipline.

By definition, marriage requires that two distinct entities become one. No matter how much in love we are, making two entirely separate individuals into a single unit is not an easy task. R. C. Sproul once said, "If you imagined your mother married to your father-in-law, and your father married to your mother-in-law, you'd have a good picture of the dynamics of marriage." I dearly love both my own parents and my in-laws, but that quote always makes me smile, for it creates an image in my mind of two preposterous unions. I don't smile nearly as wide, though, when Sproul's quote becomes plain in my own marriage.

A peaceful union is hard to achieve, and oneness is not something that happens overnight. The marriage ceremony does not magically erase the differences between husband and wife, and neither does it cancel our selfish natures. Married harmony requires instead an acceptance that conflict is bound to occur; it also requires a commitment to ongoing reconciliation—for a lifetime. That commitment creates a safe and secure place, a place where our husbands can trust us, where we can do them good—and receive good in return.

Loving Lord, I ask that You strengthen my commitment to my husband. May I not simply go through the motions of marriage, out of habit. May I actively seek to do him good, even in the bleak, cold days of our marriage's winters.

More Biblical Insight
for Your Heart

Secrets of the Proverbs 31 Woman

This devotional, offering equal parts inspiration and encouragement, will uncover the "secrets" of the Proverbs 31 woman. Each reading, tied to a theme from Proverbs 31:10–31, is rooted in biblical truth and spiritual wisdom. You will be inspired to emulate the virtues extolled in this memorable passage of scripture.

Paperback / 978-1-64352-882-3 / $12.99

Secrets of Esther
(Available December 2021)

This book will uncover the "secrets" of Esther. Each devotion, tied to a theme from the Old Testament story of Esther—beautiful queen and courageous heroine—is rooted in biblical truth and spiritual wisdom. You will be inspired to follow the example of enduring strength extolled in this memorable passage of scripture.

Paperback / 978-1-63609-087-0 / $12.99